CAMBRIDGE   MUSIC   HANDBOOKS

Verdi: *Requiem*

CAMBRIDGE MUSIC HANDBOOKS

GENERAL EDITOR Julian Rushton

Cambridge Music Handbooks provide accessible introductions to major musical works, written by the most informed commentators in the field. With the concert-goer, performer and student in mind, the books present essential information on the historical and musical context, the composition, and the performance and reception history of each work, or group of works, as well as critical discussion of the music.

Other published titles

Verdi: *Requiem*

David Rosen
Professor of Music
Cornell University

Published by the Press Syndicate of the University of Cambridge
The Pitt Building, Trumpington Street, Cambridge CB2 1RP
40 West 20th Street, New York, NY 10011–4211, USA
10 Stamford Road, Oakleigh, Melbourne 3166, Australia

First published 1995

Printed in Great Britain at the University Press, Cambridge

A catalogue record for this book is available from the British Library

Library of Congress cataloguing in publication data

Rosen, David, 1938–
Verdi, *Requiem* / David Rosen.
p. cm. – (Cambridge music handbooks)
Includes bibliographical references and index.
ISBN 0 521 39448 1 (hardback) – ISBN 0 521 39767 7 (paperback).
1. Verdi, Giuseppe, 1813–1901. Messa da Requiem.
I. Title. II. Series.
ML410.V4R73 1995
782.32′38–dc20 94–33380 CIP MN

ISBN 0 521 39448 1 hardback
ISBN 0 521 39767 7 paperback

Contents

v

Contents

Preface

With the completion of *Aida* in 1871 and the *Requiem* in 1874, Verdi, in his sixty-first year, believed that he had ended his career as a composer. There would follow only the revisions of *Simon Boccanegra* and *Don Carlos* (1881 and 1883, respectively) and his last two masterpieces, *Otello* (1887) and *Falstaff* (1893). Since the mid-1840s he had dominated without a rival the field of Italian opera, which is to say, Italian music, for opera was the only genre that mattered. His only work rivalling the operas, both in importance and quality, is the *Requiem*, probably the most frequently performed major choral work composed since the compilation of Mozart's Requiem.

In the last few decades most of the philological problems involving the *Requiem* have been resolved; and Chapters 1 and 2 summarize the current state of our knowledge about its genesis, its reception history, and contemporary performing practices. It should come as no surprise that there are few detailed analytical or critical studies of the *Requiem*: analysis of Verdi's music began in earnest only in the mid-1960s, and most energy has gone into study of the operas.[1] Chapters 3–9 provide a comprehensive view of the work, while exploring some of the critical issues raised by individual sections. One of these issues is Verdi's interpretation of the text and his reception of works that may have influenced him: the settings of Mozart, Cherubini, and Berlioz. Another aspect of its reception, the reactions of some of the major critics, is also considered in these chapters. The various pieces suggested different approaches, and I have not felt bound to adopt a uniform approach to all parts of the work.

In composing the *Requiem* Verdi made use of earlier material: most important, the *Libera me* is a revision of the movement composed in 1869 for a Requiem Mass written to commemorate the death of Rossini. The chapter on the *Libera me* includes discussion of some of the major changes, while Chapter 10 considers the two remaining revisions: the fashioning of the principal theme of the 'Lacrymosa' from a duet written for *Don Carlos* but discarded before the premiere, and the replacement of the original 'Liber scriptus' section of the *Dies iræ*, a choral fugue, with the mezzo-soprano solo known today.

The last two chapters consider two issues concerning the work as a whole: its *unità musicale* (to use Verdi's phrase) and, the central issue in its reception, its genre – specifically, the degree to which the *Requiem* is 'operatic'.

Terminology

The titles of the seven 'movements' appear in italics, while a textual incipit in quotation marks refers to individual sections or subsections: e.g., the first movement, *Requiem e Kyrie*, is composed of the 'Requiem æternam' and the 'Kyrie'; the 'Dies iræ' and 'Tuba mirum' are the first two sections of the *Dies iræ*. Verdi's entire work is usually referred to as the *Requiem* (in italics), while the genre to which it belongs, the Requiem, appears in roman type.

Scores

For all but the opening chapters the reader will need a score at hand, ideally an orchestral score furnished with bar numbers. I recommend the critical edition of the *Requiem* I prepared for *The Works of Giuseppe Verdi* (henceforth *WGV*), the only edition based primarily on the autograph score (and supplemented with other sources in the composer's hand, such as letters to his publisher and interventions made while proofreading a manuscript copy).[2] *WGV* includes the original versions of two pieces that Verdi later revised, the *Libera me* and the 'Liber scriptus' section of the *Dies iræ*.[3] A few libraries own a facsimile edition of Verdi's autograph of the *Requiem*; more accessible is the recently published facsimile of the autograph of his 1869 *Libera me* movement.[4] Both repay study but are not essential for the discussion here. There are many available recordings of the *Requiem* and even one of the complete *Messa per Rossini*, including Verdi's 1869 *Libera me* movement.[5]

Documentation

The first two chapters borrow heavily from the introduction to my edition in *WGV*, and I have not supplied references easily traced there. I have lived with the *Requiem* for many years, and it is difficult to trace the provenance of my ideas about it. I have doubtless pilfered some ideas and felicitous phrases of other writers without acknowledgment.

Introductory material in Chapters 3–9

In the texts and translations extra-liturgical text appears in square brackets (immediate repetitions of text within a section, however, are not shown). The approximate durations of the various sections or movements, usually rounded off to the nearest fifteen seconds, are based upon Verdi's metronome markings (estimating the length of the fermatas and passages with verbal indications only [e.g., *più animato*]). Even when changes of tempo are not indicated, Verdi doubtless expected some interpretative freedom rather than a rigid, metronomic tempo,[6] so to propose even an approximate duration presupposes that departures from the specified tempo will average out, that conductors will occasionally want to speed up as well as slow down.

Acknowledgments

In addition to all those who helped me prepare the critical edition of the *Requiem* and who are acknowledged there, I should like to extend my deep gratitude to Julian Rushton and Penny Souster for their perceptive editorial comments, encouragement, and nearly infinite patience.

The genesis of the Messa da Requiem per l'anniversario della morte di Manzoni 22 maggio 1874

The Messa per Rossini of 1869

Despite its connection with Alessandro Manzoni, underscored by Verdi's official title for the work,[1] the story of Verdi's *Requiem* begins with the death of Gioachino Rossini (13 November 1868) and Verdi's reaction to it: 'A great name has disappeared from the world! His was the most widespread, the most popular reputation of our time, and it was a glory of Italy! When the other one who still lives [Manzoni] is no more, what will we have left? Our ministers, and the exploits of Lissa and Custoza.' The subtext of Verdi's bitter remark is his general disgust with Italy's political and military leaders. Lissa and Custoza were humiliating, though not crucial, Italian defeats in the 1866 war for Venice, a war won on behalf of Italy by her ally, Prussia – another humiliation. Matters were no better on the domestic front: there were serious economic problems and the continuing problem of the South. 'I don't read newspapers anymore', Verdi wrote to a friend in August 1868. 'I don't want to hear about our woes anymore. There's no hope for us, when our statesmen are vain gossips.'[2]

But if Italy's statesmen and military men were a source of humiliation, her artists were a source of national pride; in particular, her music 'still carries with honour the name of Italy to every part of the world'.[3] Verdi may have been especially sensitive about this point at the time of Rossini's death, for earlier that year the Minister of Public Instruction, Emilio Broglio, in advancing an ill-advised plan to remove government support for the Conservatories, asked, 'since Rossini, that is, in the last forty years, what have we had? Four operas by Meyerbeer . . . How can such grave sterility be remedied?' Not unreasonably, Verdi took this as 'an insult to Italian musical art' and, having been named Commendatore of the Order of the Italian Crown, promptly returned the decoration. He did so not for his own sake, he told friends, but out of respect for Bellini and Donizetti, 'who filled the world with their melodies' and 'who were no longer able to defend themselves'.

Four days after Rossini's death Verdi sent a letter to Tito Ricordi, his publisher in Milan, proposing that a Requiem Mass be composed by 'the most distinguished Italian composers' and performed on the anniversary of Rossini's death. The letter was published in the Ricordi house journal, the *Gazzetta musicale di Milano* (22 November 1868), and in other Italian newspapers as well.

To honour the memory of Rossini I would wish the most distinguished Italian composers (Mercadante at the head, if only for a few bars) to compose a *Requiem Mass* to be performed on the anniversary of his death.

I would like not only the composers, but all the performing artists, in addition to lending their services, to offer also a contribution to pay the expenses.

I would like no foreign hand, no hand alien to art, no matter how powerful, to lend his assistance. In this case I would withdraw at once from the association.

The *Mass* should be performed in San Petronio, in the city of Bologna, which was Rossini's true musical home.

This *Mass* would not be an object of curiosity or of speculation; but as soon as it has been performed, it should be sealed and placed in the archives of the Liceo Musicale of that city, from which it should never be taken. Exception could perhaps be made for His anniversaries, if posterity should decide to celebrate them.

If I were in the good graces of the Holy Father, I would beg him to allow, at least this once, women to take part in the performance of this music, but since I am not, it would be best to find a person more suitable than I to achieve this end.[4]

It would be best to set up a committee of intelligent men to take charge of the arrangements for this performance, and especially to choose the composers, assign the pieces, and watch over the general form of the work.

The composition (however good the individual numbers may be) will necessarily lack musical unity; but if it is wanting in this respect it will serve nonetheless to show how great in all of us is the veneration for that man whose loss the whole world mourns.

The first question raised by this problematic document concerns the choice of a Requiem Mass as a means of commemorating Rossini's death. Verdi was anticlerical and, at least in this period, almost certainly an agnostic. Furthermore the period was one of intense conflict between Church and State: in 1864 Pius IX had issued the reactionary Syllabus of Errors; two years later the Italian parliament passed a law declaring 'that almost all the religious orders and congregations should have their houses dissolved and their goods confiscated'.[5] Most important perhaps was the State's continuing effort to wrest Rome from the papal power, accomplished only in 1870.

The Requiem Mass, however, was considered as much a public and political ritual as a religious one, as Cherubini's C-minor Requiem and Berlioz's *Grande messe des morts* attest (both were designed for political celebrations).

Many of the commemorations of Rossini's death included performances of a Requiem Mass, whether works of established pedigree (Mozart's, Cherubini's D-minor Requiem) or not.[6] Verdi's decision to propose a Requiem Mass as the means to honour Rossini in a national ceremony is therefore understandable.

Had Verdi's ambitious project come to fruition, his idealistic but stringent conditions would have added moral prestige to it; as it turned it out, they may have sealed its fate. His insistence that the composition should not be an 'object of speculation' shifted the responsibility for organization and financing from impresario and publisher to a committee, and to the composers and performers themselves, who were asked not only to contribute their labour but also to subsidize the performance. Even other sources of disinterested support were ruled out: from foreign hands, from hands alien to art. As a supposedly national event, it competed with countless local celebrations. And finally, when insuperable difficulties arose – the immediate cause being the refusal of the impresario of the Bologna Teatro Comunale to make his singers, chorus, and orchestra available – Verdi's continued insistence that the event must take place in San Petronio on the anniversary of Rossini's death made it impossible to perform the work at all.

The defensive stance of the final paragraph of Verdi's letter testifies to serious doubts about the aesthetic quality of the composition, in particular its lack of *unità musicale*. However, he would consistently maintain that the aesthetic value of the *Messa per Rossini* was less important than its value as an essentially patriotic ritual: 'What does it matter, then, that the composition lacks unity, that the contribution of this or that composer is more or less beautiful? . . . It's enough that the day comes, the ceremony takes place, and, in short, that the *Historic fact* – mark well, the *Historic fact* – exists.'

A committee was duly formed,[7] and in early June 1869 it promulgated a prospectus with the composers, their assignments, and – in an attempt to minimize the artistic anarchy entailed by the composite nature of the work – the resources, key, and tempo of each piece. Verdi's assignment was the final movement, *Libera me*. Although it seems that it was the committee – not Verdi – that took primary responsibility for selecting the composers and designing the large-scale structure of the *Messa per Rossini*,[8] Verdi was pleased with the results: 'it seems to me that it was done with the greatest judgment regarding the division, form, and distribution of the pieces'. As we shall see, the prospectus of the *Messa per Rossini* may have influenced him in planning some aspects of his 1874 *Messa da Requiem*.

On 1 August 1869 Verdi asked Tito Ricordi to send him music paper so that he could write his piece. He had probably already made preliminary sketches, for only four days later he could inform Giulio, 'My piece is almost finished and lacks only a bit of *polishing* and the orchestration.' And on 20 August he announced, 'Tomorrow I shall send my piece for the Messa a Rossini: *Libera me, Domine.* In case this ceremony does not take place . . . I urge you to see that the piece is well taken care of and returned to me.' There was good reason for Verdi's concern. Although all of the composers finished their compositions in time, the proposed ceremony came to naught, and the *Messa per Rossini* had to wait until 1988 for its premiere.

Towards the *Messa da Requiem*

When did Verdi decide to build a complete Requiem around the already composed *Libera me*? It was once thought that he had continued to work on the composition, completing three-quarters of it (the *Requiem e Kyrie*, the entire *Dies iræ*, and, naturally, the *Libera me*) by early 1871 and the whole work by the autumn of 1872.[9] But the evidence suggests that Verdi did not take up the work again until 1873.

In the year and a half following the cancellation of the Bologna ceremony Ricordi attempted to persuade Verdi to allow the Mass to be performed in some other context. Verdi would have none of it: with the cancellation of the Rossini commemoration, the work had lost all significance. Nonetheless, taking the position that he was merely one of the contributors, he stopped short of making non-negotiable demands and even recognized the possibility that the Mass might be performed elsewhere. Consider, for example, his reply to a proposal made by the committee at the end of 1869: '. . . allow me to ask you *sotto voce*: is this Mass such that it can stand the comparison with the other celebrated Requiem Masses, which perhaps aren't even the masterpieces that the world pretends to believe? If this were so, I too would be reconciled with the idea of seeing it performed.' And again: 'Conclusion. Can the new *Mass* compete with those of Mozart, Cherubini, etc. . . . with the *Stabat*, with the *Petite Messe*? Yes? Give it. No? Then *Pax vobis*.'[10]

Difficult conditions, but Verdi seems to have been willing to allow the committee's decision to rest on the artistic merits of the composition. It seems unlikely that he would have begun to construct a Requiem around the *Libera me*, if it seemed possible that the *Messa per Rossini*, crowned by this very same piece, might soon receive a public performance.

Matters came to a head in January 1871, when the committee, urged by Verdi 'to conclude the business of this Mass once and for all', decided to 'examine the entire *Mass* with the most scrupulous rigour . . . to see if it is a composition that can risk a theatre performance'. This is the context for Alberto Mazzucato's well-known letter of 2 February 1871, written after his examination of Verdi's *Libera me*: 'You, my dear Maestro, have written the most beautiful, the greatest, and most colossally poetic page that can be imagined.'

Verdi responded two days later in an important letter:

. . . those words of yours would almost have instilled in me the desire to finish, later, the entire *Mass*: so much the more so because with some more development I would find myself already having finished the *Requiem* and the *Dies iræ*, of which the reprise in the *Libera* is already composed. Consider then, and regret, what dreadful consequences your praise could have – but do not worry: it is a temptation that will pass like so many others. I do not like useless things. There are so many, many *Requiem Masses*!!! It is useless to add one more.

It is hard to see how some writers could interpret this as evidence that Verdi had continued to work on a Requiem: the letter says only that *if* he were ever to complete it, he would borrow material for the 'Requiem æternam' and 'Dies iræ' from the 1869 *Libera me*, so that the appearance of that material there, in the last movement of the *Requiem*, would function as a reprise. The fate of the *Messa per Rossini* was soon sealed, and the *coup de grâce* was given in August 1871 when the committee returned one of the contributions to its composer (Federico Ricci).

Verdi's autograph score of the *Libera me* was returned to him on 21 April 1873. He surely would not have started work on completing a Requiem before then: since the *Libera me* was to provide material for the first two movements, he would have asked Ricordi for that score the moment he decided to do so.[11] Furthermore, it seems likely that the score was returned at his request, or at least after hints that he was contemplating returning to the work. It can hardly be a coincidence that, two weeks earlier, a note signed 'Un dilettante' (but probably planted by Ricordi) had appeared in the *Gazzetta musicale di Milano* (6 April issue): 'Why could not Verdi give new life to sacred music, now fallen to such a low point?' All this suggests the puzzling conclusion that Verdi's decision to complete the *Messa da Requiem* may have been reached a month before Alessandro Manzoni's death on 22 May 1873.

It is understandable that Verdi would wish to honour Manzoni with a Requiem Mass. Verdi regarded Manzoni and Rossini as pillars of Italian glory, and it is for this reason, rather than any deep personal attachment to Rossini, that Verdi initiated the *Messa per Rossini* project. But in addition to the esteem he accorded to Manzoni as a quasi-political figure – as a world-renowned Italian – Verdi felt a great personal reverence towards the man as writer and patriot. At the age of sixteen he first read *I promessi sposi*, the novel he later described as 'not only the greatest book of our epoch, but one of the greatest ever to emerge from a human brain'. The novel, in its revised, tuscanized form, was also critical in the establishment of a common vernacular language for the emerging Italian nation. In his teens he composed settings of Manzoni's Ode 'Il cinque maggio' and several choruses from his tragedies *Il conte di Carmagnola* and *Adelchi*.[12] It was only in June 1868 that the two men finally met, the meeting arranged by Clara Maffei. Verdi's letters reveal an uncharacteristic awe and even more uncharacteristic quasi-hagiographical imagery:

What could I say to you of Manzoni? How to explain the very sweet, indefinable, new sensation produced in me, in the presence of that Saint, as you call him? I would have knelt before him, if men could be worshipped. They say it must not be done, and so be it: although we venerate on altars many who did not have the talent or the virtues of Manzoni, and [here Verdi's more typical voice returns] who indeed were downright rascals. When you see him kiss his hand and tell him for me all my veneration.[13]

It therefore comes as no surprise that Verdi wanted to commemorate Manzoni's death, but one wonders why he seems to have made his decision to complete the Requiem – or at least begun to give serious consideration to doing so – even before that event occurred. He probably did not become aware of the writer's failing health until early May. By 10 May the newspapers had referred to a serious blow inflicted upon his mind by the recent death of his son Pietro; a few days later they reported that he was suddenly stricken with paralysis and that his life was in danger. The end came on 22 May 1873.[14]

However, even if Verdi had no information about Manzoni's health in April 1873, he *did* know that he was eighty-eight years old. It hardly required medical reports to know that a Requiem would prove useful, sooner rather than later. And yet Verdi might possibly have decided to complete the composition for reasons independent of Manzoni. He believed that with *Aida* he had taken his leave of the hurly-burly of the theatre; yet he did not want to, or could not, renounce composing altogether. The string quartet was composed in the previous month, and, given his view that German music is instrumental while Italian – 'la nostra' – is vocal, it is not surprising that he next turned his hand to sacred vocal music. If *Aida* was to have been his *Guillaume Tell*, the *Requiem* would be his *Stabat Mater* or *Petite Messe*. The parallel with Rossini's career cannot have escaped him.

Verdi learned of Manzoni's death through a telegram from Clara Maffei, and on the following day he wrote to Ricordi: 'I am profoundly saddened by the death of our Great Man! But I shall not come to Milan, for I would not have the heart to attend his funeral. I will come soon to visit his grave, alone and unseen, and perhaps (after further reflection, after having weighed my strength) to propose something to honour his memory.' And his letter to Clara Maffei on the day of the funeral picks up the thread begun with the death of Rossini five years earlier: 'Now it is all ended! And with Him ends the purest, the most holy, the highest of our glories.' This mixture of nostalgia and pessimism makes plausible the view of some writers that, in bidding farewell to Manzoni, Verdi was also writing a 'Requiem for the Risorgimento' and marking the passing of a whole generation and a whole tradition.[15]

At the beginning of June Verdi came to Milan to visit Manzoni's grave; on 3 June he wrote to Ricordi:

I too would like to demonstrate what affection and veneration I bore and bear that Great Man who is no more, and whom Milan has so worthily honoured. I would like to set to music a *Mass for the Dead* to be performed next year for the anniversary of his death. The *Mass* would have rather vast dimensions, and besides a large orchestra and a large chorus, it would also require – I cannot be specific now – four or five principal singers.

Do you think the City would assume the expense of the performance? I would have the copying of the music done at my expense, and I myself would conduct the performance both at the rehearsals and in church. If you believe this possible speak to the Mayor about it . . . you can consider this letter of mine binding.

The Mayor of Milan gratefully accepted Verdi's offer. Verdi in turn assured him that no thanks were owed him for 'It is an impulse, or better, a need of the heart that impels me to honour, insofar as I can, this Great Man, whom I so admired as a writer and venerated as a man, model of virtue and of patriotism!' And so Verdi was formally bound to complete his *Messa da Requiem*.

The chronology of composition

The Verdis spent most of the summer of 1873 in Paris and, according to Giuseppina Verdi, the composer worked 'un pochino' on the *Requiem* in August there. They were back at Sant'Agata by 14 September, and for about a month Verdi '[didn't do] anything but stroll around in the fields, eat, and sleep'. 'But now', he wrote on 19 October, 'if the weather turns bad, as it seems it will, I'll be forced to stay inside, and I'll take up my *Mass* again. I'd like to finish it before going to Genoa; at least I'd like to finish the creative part.'

7

By 'la parte creativa' Verdi meant the skeleton score; elaborate and imaginative as much of the orchestration is, he still viewed it as secondary.[16] After Verdi visited Milan in late January 1874, Clara Maffei observed: 'I have never seen Verdi work with so much love on a work and lavish such care upon it.' His enthusiasm for the project, though cloaked in irony, is also evident in his comments to his friends Camille Du Locle and Giuseppe Piroli. To the former he wrote:

I'm working on my *Mass* and doing so with great pleasure. I feel as if I've become a solid citizen and am no longer the public's clown who, with a big *tamburone* and bass drum, shouts 'come, come, step right up', etc., etc. As you can imagine, when I hear operas spoken of now, my conscience is scandalized, and I immediately make the sign of the Cross!! . . . What do you say to that? Am I not an edifying example?

On 7 March he told Piroli, 'I've been here since the beginning of the year and haven't done anything but write notes upon notes for the greater glory of God, and perhaps for the future annoyance of my fellow man. But be that as it may, the music is now finished, and I'm pleased that I've done it.' Verdi probably meant that he had finished a continuity draft or skeleton score of the entire work, for it was not until 30 March that he sent off the first two movements of the work, with additional instalments on 9 April (all of the remaining movements, except the *Offertorio*, 'in which [he wanted] to make a small change at the beginning'), and 15 April. On 16 April he informed Piroli that he had been 'very busy and worried over that *devil* of a Mass, which is finally finished'.

Precompositional decisions

There were a number of basic decisions that Verdi needed to reach before putting pen to paper. With the exception of the *Libera me,* composed in 1869, Verdi had not tried his hand at sacred music for more than thirty years. It would have been natural for him to seek to acquaint (or reacquaint) himself with some of the standard settings of the Requiem Mass, as one contemporary account claims:

Verdi, who knows what is due to his reputation, and leaves nothing to chance, took care to make himself acquainted at Paris with all the Requiems written by the great masters. He read Mozart's, Berlioz's, and Cherubini's two, as well as others less celebrated, and came to the conclusion that the *Dies Iræ* had never been musically treated in the exact spirit of the Latin text.

Whether or not one credits this account, a letter of December 1869 (see p. 4) implies some familiarity with the Requiems of Mozart and Cherubini and suggests that Verdi regarded them as the most eminent examples of the genre. To what extent he was familiar with the Berlioz *Grande messe des morts* remains an open question; although he apparently did not own the score, he did own Alberto Mazzucato's Italian translation of Berlioz's *Grande traité d'instrumentation et d'orchestration modernes*, which includes three excerpts from the *Grande messe*: the 'Tuba mirum', and portions of the 'Rex tremendæ' and the 'Hostias'.[17] Moreover, while Verdi never saw his colleagues' contributions to the *Messa per Rossini*, he had conserved his copy of the prospectus – a document which he had praised warmly.[18]

Even though Verdi did not require the services of a librettist, he still needed to decide upon the liturgical text to be set to music rather than relegated to performance as plainchant. For in the Requiem Mass, unlike the Mass Ordinary, there is no standard text common to all polyphonic settings. For example, while Mozart's Requiem includes Introit, Kyrie, Sequence, Offertory, Sanctus, Agnus Dei, and Communion, Cherubini's two Requiems also include a Gradual and a 'Pie Jesu Domine' positioned between the *Sanctus* and *Agnus Dei* (an item found in the Requiems of Dvořák and Fauré as well). For the text of the Mass itself, the committee for the *Messa per Rossini* followed the example of Mozart, incorporating the Introit and Kyrie into a single movement, dividing the *Dies iræ* into about a half-dozen sections, and allocating a separate movement for the Communion (Cherubini and Berlioz incorporated it into the *Agnus Dei*). On the other hand, it did not allot a separate movement to the 'Benedictus' or specify fugal treatment of the 'Osanna'. The committee added as a final movement the responsory from the Burial Service (Absolution ceremony): *Libera me*, a movement not uncommon in nineteenth-century Italian Requiems. The text Verdi adopted is identical with that of the *Messa per Rossini*, including, of course, the *Libera me* already composed.[19]

Verdi also followed the example of the *Messa per Rossini* regarding the role that soloists would play. Neither of the Cherubini works employs soloists, and Berlioz limited himself to a single tenor in the *Sanctus*, offering the option of assigning the 'solo' to ten tenors in unison. The four soloists in Mozart's Requiem have few substantial assignments and generally appear as a quartet. But the *Messa per Rossini* and Verdi's *Requiem* are 'Cantata-Masses', where entire sections or movements are assigned to individual soloists and to ensembles drawn from the pool of soloists, sometimes with the participation of the chorus.[20] This is an important feature not found in the Requiems of Mozart, Cherubini, or Berlioz, or, for that matter, in the remainder of Verdi's own sacred music. The *Messa per Rossini* calls for five soloists, but Verdi eventually settled on four.

The prospectus for the *Messa per Rossini* limited the orchestra to strings, piccolo, two flutes, two oboes, English horn, two clarinets, bass clarinet, four bassoons, four horns, four trumpets, three trombones and ophicleide, timpani, gran cassa, and organ.[21] In writing his 1869 *Libera me*, Verdi accepted these limitations, also forgoing the English horn and bass clarinet – instruments in wide use in the opera house but not part of the standard symphonic orchestra – and organ, an instrument obviously associated with the church and, indeed, frequently used in his operas to evoke 'Church Music'. Although Verdi had a free hand in writing his own *Messa da Requiem*, he adopted the same orchestra he had used in the 1869 movement, but with the addition of four off-stage trumpets for the 'Tuba mirum' section of the *Dies iræ* and the substitution of a third flute for piccolo in the *Agnus Dei*.

Borrowings and revisions

The relationship of the 1869 *Libera me* and its counterpart in the 1874 *Messa da Requiem* had been a subject of controversy until a manuscript of the *Messa per Rossini* came to light about twenty-five years ago, demonstrating that the 1874 *Libera me* is a revealing but not radical revision of the earlier piece.[22] We encounter borrowed material of a different kind in the 'Lacrymosa' section of the *Dies iræ*. Verdi drew its theme from a duet composed for *Don Carlos* but removed before its 11 March 1867 premiere at the Paris Opéra. Since the number had never been performed he could recycle it for the *Requiem* with impunity.

Verdi's autograph shows many signs of 'pentimenti', but most of these concern details: he must already have prepared a continuity draft and, of course, for the *Libera me* and music derived from it, he had the completed 1869 score at hand. Although Verdi made a handful of further small revisions during his cursory proofreading of a manuscript copy of the orchestral score, the only revision that can be securely dated after the 1874 premiere is the replacement of the original setting of the 'Liber scriptus' section (see pp. 13–14).

2

The premiere, subsequent performance history, and performing practices

Church and State

Verdi's *Messa da Requiem* was first performed in church as part of a liturgical ceremony – a curious hybrid in which the 'movements' of Verdi's Roman-rite Mass alternated with Ambrosian-rite plainchant. 'While Verdi conducted the performance of the *Requiem*, Monsignor Calvi celebrated a "dry mass" [*Messa secca*], that is, without the consecration of the bread and wine.'[1] His primary criterion in selecting the church seems to have been its acoustics: he passed over the Cathedral, San Fedele (the church that Manzoni frequented), and Santa Maria delle Grazie in favour of San Marco. Ricordi informed Verdi that the parish priest, 'Don Michele Mongeri, is a cultivated man, likeable, and liberal, although religious . . . You will get on very well with him.' It fell to Mongeri to obtain permission from the Archbishop to allow women to participate in the performance. This was eventually granted, provided that 'all possible precautions [be taken] that the women be hidden by a grating, [placed] off to one side, or something similar'. Indeed, at the San Marco performance – but not subsequent performances – the female choristers wore 'a full black dress with the head covered by an ample mourning veil'.

When Verdi first offered to compose and conduct the *Requiem*, the Mayor accepted without hesitation, but when the proposal was deliberated by the Milan City Council on 24 February 1874, two councillors questioned the expenses, while another argued that it was inappropriate for the City to 'associate itself with religious ceremonies, with a Mass to be celebrated, and for which one would need to choose the church and ask permission of the Archbishop'. One of the fifty-five councillors present was Arrigo Boito, who offered a motion – 'approved with a nearly unanimous vote' – that the City administration gratefully accept Verdi's proposal and provide for its realization. The opposition to municipal funding of the performance of the Mass must be understood in the context of extreme tension between Church and State at this time, only four years after the annexation of Rome against the

11

will of Pius IX. A few months later the same anticlerical councillor would successfully oppose a proposal to purchase the house of Manzoni for a museum – the anticlerical faction did not hold Manzoni in high esteem[2] – and would play a role in prohibiting the procession of St. Ambrose on the grounds that demonstrations and disorders might ensue. The ban on the procession could have had consequences for the church performance of Verdi's *Requiem*: according to one newspaper, it had been rumoured that as a reprisal the church authorities would prohibit the Mass.

Financial concerns and reception of the premiere

In his proposal for the *Messa per Rossini* Verdi was adamant that the work should not become an object of speculation, but the situation was very different with the *Messa da Requiem*. Far from wanting the score sealed up in the archives, Verdi engaged in extended negotiations with his publishers, Ricordi and, in Paris, Escudier. For the sale of rights, Verdi received 35,000 francs from Ricordi and 15,000 francs from Escudier; in addition he would also receive substantial royalties.[3] Furthermore, the premiere at San Marco was followed by three performances at La Scala with the same soloists: Teresa Stolz (soprano), Maria Waldmann (mezzo-soprano), Giuseppe Capponi (tenor), and Ormondo Maini (bass). Verdi directed the performance on 25 May, Franco Faccio those of 27 and 29 May. The profits, 16,364.19 lire, were divided equally between the city of Milan and the Ricordi firm,[4] Ricordi in turn dividing his share equally with Verdi. The composer thus received 4,091.05.[5]

In general, the work was received enthusiastically by the press. One exception was the virulent report of Hans von Bülow filed on the eve of the performance and printed in the *Allgemeine Zeitung*. Referring to the work as an 'opera in ecclesiastical costume [Oper im Kirchengewande]', he wrote:

Some furtive glances into the new lucubration of the author of *Il trovatore* and *La traviata* have really not made us anxious to enjoy this *Festival*, though we cannot refuse the composer our testimony that he has taken pains with his task. Thus, among other pieces, the final fugue, despite many things worthy only of a student, of much that is insipid and disagreeable, is a work of such industry that many German musicians will experience great surprise at it. But, as a rule, the dominant style is that of his last manner [that of *Aida*], a style of which a clever Viennese teacher of singing said 'that it was improved to its disadvantage'.[6]

After reading the score Brahms reportedly said, 'Bülow has disgraced himself for all time; only a genius could write such a work.' Nearly twenty years later von Bülow would finally recant and receive Verdi's carefully worded absolution. Nonetheless, the issue of the work's appropriateness for the church – whether the work was an 'Oper im Kirchengewande' – has remained a constant theme in discussion of the *Messa da Requiem* down to the present day (see Chapter 12).

Performances to 1879

Immediately after the first performances in Milan, Verdi took the work to Paris, where, between 9 and 22 June, it received seven performances. He was pleased with the reception: 'twenty more performances – with a full house – could have been given'. However, during the coming months there were other performances, projected or realized, that he did not welcome: 'At Ferrara an assassin of a band director arranged the Mass for Manzoni for military band and had it performed in an arena! . . . There's more: at Bologna they too are threatening to perform it publicly with soloists, chorus, and Pianos!!' The threat of pirated performances was even greater outside Europe. For example, the United States had 'no treaties with any country regarding intellectual property', a Ricordi employee complained to Verdi, and 'they habitually orchestrate any work [from printed piano-vocal scores]'. To ensure that the work be performed with Verdi's orchestration, Ricordi sold performance materials to the impresario Strakosch for the American premiere (Academy of Music, New York, 17 November 1874), with a chorus of 150 and an orchestra of eighty, directed by Emanuele Muzio, Verdi's friend and former pupil.[7] One sympathizes with Strakosch's claim to the American premiere, as the performance in New York's St. Ann's Church a few weeks earlier (25 October) had a chorus of twenty and organ accompaniment.

Verdi and Ricordi were careful to control the quality of the initial performances: in 1874 only Milan, Paris, and New York heard authorized renditions, conducted by Verdi, Faccio, or Muzio. In 1875 Verdi undertook a *tournée*, taking the work to Paris, London, and Vienna.

The 'Liber scriptus' rewritten: performances in London, May 1875

The version of the *Requiem* performed on 22 May 1874 was the one known today, with a single, important exception: the 'Liber scriptus' section of the *Dies iræ* was a fugue for four-part chorus and orchestra, rather than a solo for mezzo-soprano. On 21 November 1874 Verdi informed Waldmann of his desire to replace the fugal setting with a solo for her: 'in case it doesn't suit you or if it would be a nuisance to learn a new little piece, I can think up something else [i.e., another way of replacing the fugue]'. She was naturally delighted with his suggestion, and on 6 February he sent Ricordi the new piece. Since the *Requiem* had already been heard in Paris, Verdi suggested that they postpone performing the new composition until after the performances there: 'You know that the first impressions of the public are always dreadfully powerful [*terribili*], and even if that piece was effective everyone would say, "*It was better as it was before*".' He also was concerned that there would not be adequate time for her to study the new work, which was 'easy – very easy – as notes and as music, but you know that there are always intentions that one must think about'. The new 'Liber scriptus' received its premiere on 15 May 1875 in London's Royal Albert Hall.[8] For the new piece Verdi received 2,500 lire from Ricordi, 1,000 francs from Escudier.

The *tournée* concluded in Vienna, where the *Requiem*, alternating with performances of *Aida*, was first presented on 11 June. Verdi would again direct the *Requiem* in Paris (at the Théâtre Italien, the first performance on 30 May 1876), in Cologne (during the Lower Rhine Music Festival, 21 May 1877), and finally once more at La Scala (30 June 1879), a performance, suggested by Verdi himself, to benefit the victims of the flood that had devastated large portions of northern Italy.

Later performance history

The *Requiem* is so firmly enshrined in the canon now that it is difficult to believe that it was not always a repertory piece. The work was widely performed in the first few years of its life: by the end of 1875 it had been performed in Italy (Milan, Venice, Trieste, Florence), France, England, Austria, Germany, Belgium, Egypt, Spain, Hungary, the United States, and Argentina. But performances then declined sharply.[9] At La Scala, for example, after the initial run in 1874 and the benefit for the flood victims in 1879, the next four series of performances were all associated with commemorations: the tenth anniversary of Manzoni's death (1883), the first anniversary of Verdi's death (1902), the centenary of his birth (1913), and the fiftieth anniversary of Manzoni's death (1923). Starting with the mid-1930s the frequency of performances increased, and after 1944 there was an average of about one series every other year. None of the twenty-seven major American orchestras surveyed in Kate Hevner Mueller's repertoire study performed Verdi's *Requiem* before the 1930s.[10] Although the so-called 'Verdi Renaissance' began in the mid-1920s, it may have been only in the 1930s or even later that the *Requiem* entered the canon.

The performing forces

Discussing the voices of nineteenth-century singers is a risky venture, easily degenerating into impressionistic gossip. Nonetheless, some familiarity with the singers that the composer chose to interpret his work – especially those he had in mind as he created it – can help to explain various compositional choices and may also provide useful suggestions about appropriate present-day interpreters. From the outset Verdi knew that Teresa Stolz would be the soprano soloist, and the part was designed to take advantage of her remarkable qualities. Her voice 'extended securely from g to c♯³'. According to one contemporary account, 'She takes a tone and sustains it until it seems that her respiration is quite exhausted and then she has only commenced to hold it. The tones are as fine and clearly cut as a diamond, and sweet as a silver bell; but the power she gives a high C is something amazing.'[11]

Verdi gives us information about qualities required for success in the *Requiem* by pointing out the lack of those very qualities in Antonietta Fricci, whose voice had a limited upper register and a mezzo-soprano colour. 'I don't think that Fricci can manage to sustain the high notes sufficiently. Even at Paris the two most immediate and sensational effects are in those two phrases where a high c is sustained at length.' And again, 'If Fricci is doing badly in *Aida*, she'll do worse in the Mass, where security of voice and intonation and the ability to sustain very long phrases [*fiati lunghissimi*] are even more necessary than in *Aida*.' Paradoxically, Fricci seems to have been the singer Verdi had in mind for the 1869 *Libera me*, and some of the revisions of that movement that he made five years later, especially the raising of the tessitura, were due to the differences between the vocal qualities of the two singers.

In late July 1873 Maria Waldmann offered to participate in the performance of the *Requiem*, and Verdi eagerly accepted. Although it required intense, even acrimonious negotiations to free her from conflicting commitments, Verdi doubtless conceived the second female part with her in mind, and she would take part in all but one series of performances that he directed. While most operatic historians classify her as a mezzo-soprano – her roles did include Amneris, Azucena, and Eboli – Verdi thought otherwise: 'Waldmann, for example, can do all the high a²s and b♭²s she wants, but will always be a contralto.'[12]

There was little discussion about the choice of male soloists. Verdi's principal criterion for the tenor was an attractive vocal quality, rather than intelligence, musical artistry, or acting abilities – virtues he would have insisted upon for an operatic role. His ideal would have been Giuseppe Fancelli, renowned for his beautiful voice and monumental stupidity. Verdi once characterized him as 'beautiful voice, but a pumpkinhead'. About another tenor, he would write: '[Roberto] Stagno is a handsome youth, good actor, and he gets good effects on f^1, g^1, a^1, bb^1, and even $b\natural^1$, but his voice is extremely bad. His good qualities are therefore useless for the *Mass*.'

What forces should be adopted for a 'historically informed' performance of Verdi's *Requiem*? There is no reason to give special weight to the performing forces used at the premiere, and the seven 'productions' directed by Verdi from 1874 to 1879 offer a vast range of *ipso facto* 'authentic' sizes for the orchestra and chorus. However, most employed a total of 200 to 280 performers, generally with a chorus ranging from about 9 per cent to 50 per cent larger than the orchestra, but not overwhelming it. The orchestra was significantly larger than the typical opera orchestra; it consisted of at least 100, including 29 winds and percussion, and a minimum of 71 strings; for example, the premiere at San Marco Church and La Scala (May 1874), chorus 120, orchestra 100 or 110; Vienna (June 1875), chorus 150, orchestra 100; La Scala (June 1879), chorus 150, orchestra 130. But on two occasions Verdi used much larger forces: the performance at the Lower Rhine Music Festival in Cologne (May 1877) had a chorus of about 500 and an orchestra of 200, and that in the capacious Royal Albert Hall (May 1875) a chorus of 1200, an orchestra of 150, with, according to one newspaper report, Dr. Stainer at the organ.

Other issues of performing practice

Many conductors today perform the *Requiem* as though it were a symphony: from beginning to end, unbroken by applause or an intermission. In the concert performances directed by Verdi, however, an intermission followed the *Dies iræ*, and Verdi not only tolerated applause but frequently acknowledged it by granting encores: the 'Recordare', 'Hostias', and especially the *Agnus Dei* were often repeated.

A performance of the *Requiem* in 1874 would have differed in many respects from one heard today. The orchestra, playing from parts with non-uniform articulation and perhaps never having had a purely orchestral rehearsal – Verdi regarded them as a waste of time – would probably have sounded much less 'disciplined' than its counterpart today. There were differences in playing technique – for example, far less use of vibrato[13] – and differences in the construction of the instruments themselves: Italian trombones were equipped with valves, rather than slides; some of the contrabasses would have been the Italian three-stringed instrument tuned A – d – g;[14] the lowest brass part was scored for the now-obsolete ophicleide.[15]

One of the most important issues – especially for vocal music – was the 'diapason'. At the time of the composition of the *Requiem*, Verdi insisted upon adopting a tuning where $a^1 = 435$ Hz, the *diapason normal* adopted legally in France in 1859, and would later express a slight preference for 432 Hz – rather than today's cruel 440 Hz or higher.

The thorniest issue of all is performance style. Verdi's desire to distance the *Requiem* from opera affected his views about how the work should be performed: 'One mustn't sing this Mass in the way one sings an opera, and therefore phrasing and dynamics that may be fine in the theatre won't satisfy me at all, not at all.' And he was pleased with the 1876 performances in Paris because he was able to obtain a 'less theatrical' interpretation than in Italy.

An especially revealing account of Verdi's performance of the *Requiem*, written by August Guckeisen, was published the day after Verdi conducted it in Cologne.[16] He noted the use of 'a certain degree of rubato', which is also supported by Verdi's praise of the orchestra and chorus of the 1875 Vienna performance: 'What a good orchestra and what good choruses! how elastic they are and how well they let themselves be led.'[17] On the other hand, Guckeisen remarked that 'his [fermatas] are kept as short as possible, never destroying the sense of rhythm'. The performance apparently had a sharper character than Guckeisen was accustomed to: 'the entire performance seemed strange, in the sense that it was far removed from our national sensibility . . . Verdi chose much sharper, more strident nuances than is customary in Germany'.

3

Requiem e Kyrie

Requiem e Kyrie: A quattro voci (Soprano, Mezzo-Soprano, Tenore e Basso) e Coro. A minor, A major; 140 bars (6'15"–6'45")

Like Mozart, Verdi set the 'Requiem æternam' (i.e., the Introit of the Requiem Mass) and 'Kyrie' as two discrete but linked numbers (Cherubini and Berlioz had integrated the two liturgical texts into a single movement).

'Requiem æternam': chorus – bb. 1–77. Orchestra: strings (all muted but the contrabasses). A minor; Andante, **C** (♩ = 80); Poco più (♩ = 88); Come prima (♩ = 80); 77 bars (*c.* 3'45")

Antiphon:	Requiem æternam dona eis, Domine: et lux perpetua luceat eis.	Grant them eternal rest, O Lord, and let perpetual light shine upon them.
Psalm:	Te decet hymnus, Deus, in Sion, et tibi reddetur votum in Jerusalem: exaudi orationem meam, ad te omnis caro veniet.	A hymn is owed to Thee in Zion, Lord, and a vow shall be returned to Thee in Jerusalem. Hear my prayer, to Thee shall come all flesh.
Antiphon:	Requiem æternam dona eis, Domine: et lux perpetua luceat eis.	Grant them eternal rest, O Lord, and let perpetual light shine upon them.

Fig. 3.1 'Requiem æternam' text

Verdi followed the ABA structure suggested by the liturgical text: the two statements of the 'Requiem æternam' antiphon, flanking the sharply contrasting Psalm verse 'Te decet hymnus', are virtually identical until the end of the second statement, the link into the 'Kyrie'. He drew the antiphon from the corresponding passage in the 1869 *Libera me*, abbreviating and arranging for string orchestra the original setting for soprano soloist and chorus *a voci sole*.[1]

The role of the chorus in the antiphon is limited to syllabic declamation, mainly on *sotto voce* repeated notes or chords.

The movement begins quietly, with the cellos playing an evocative distillation of the theme which follows in the violins, setting in relief the outlined octave of that theme. The passage that follows ('dona eis, Domine') has contrapuntal aspirations that immediately distance the work from the world of opera: a chain of suspensions in five real parts. The cross relations and the high level of dissonance act as a foil for the following passage: at the phrase 'et lux perpetua' there is a sudden turn to the parallel major – a 'soft ray of sunlight' according to the supposed arch-formalist Eduard Hanslick – a *subito ppp* dynamic after the preceding crescendo, and a sudden reduction in the dissonance level.[2] Verdi interprets the image 'Requiem æternam' as tragic, with 'lux perpetua' offering solace. The two images are musically related: the 'lux perpetua' theme expands the octave descent of the opening idea into a ninth, a shape common to a number of important themes in the *Requiem* (see p. 81 and Ex. 11.1 below). Even before the sentence is completed, however, the music turns back to the minor mode and cadences deceptively into F major, the key of the next section.

The Psalm verse, 'Te decet hymnus' (bb. 28–55), is the first of several passages for unaccompanied voices, and the only one scored for chorus alone. With the exception of the 39-bar 'Requiem æternam' section of the *Libera me*, it is also the longest. It starts out with a point of imitation with entries at one- or two-bar intervals, but, typically, abandons imitative texture once all the voices have entered.[3] The *a cappella* scoring, imitation, and severe melodic material – all evoking the *stile antico* – again serve to distance Verdi's *Requiem* from the profane world of opera: Verdi makes the point early on. The opening motive – the only distinctive material in the passage – belongs to the second important family of themes in the *Requiem* (see p. 81 and Ex. 11.2). The antiphon repeats, without the introductory five-bar phrase, and, adding the woodwinds (minus piccolo) and horns in the final bars, leads to the 'Kyrie'.

'Kyrie': the four soloists and chorus – bb. 78–140. Orchestra: woodwinds, horns, timpani, and strings. A major; Animando un poco; **C**; 63 bars (2'30"–3'00")

Kyrie eleison, Christe eleison,	Lord have mercy, Christ have mercy,
Kyrie eleison,	Lord have mercy,
Christe eleison, Kyrie eleison.	Christ have mercy, Lord have mercy.

Fig. 3.2 'Kyrie eleison' text

19

In both the prospectus for the *Messa per Rossini* and the original printed libretto for Verdi's *Messa da Requiem* the text is presented in a five-part, rather than the traditional tripartite, arrangement. Verdi's setting follows neither plan: after close alternation of 'Kyrie' and 'Christe' as the soloists enter one by one, there are four subsections setting 'Kyrie', 'Christe', 'Kyrie', finally ending with 'Christe'. Verdi seems to have been guided primarily by the criterion of declamation: at least after the opening, passages built upon the principal motive or close derivations of it are set to 'Kyrie eleison', which fits the motive better. In the 'Kyrie' the music traces its own expressive plot virtually independent of the text.

The opening of the 'Kyrie' marks a new stage in the discourse: the winds enter, the strings remove their mutes and initiate a steady eighth-note pulsation, and the tenor soloist enters with a lyrical melody over an instrumental countermelody progressing in contrary motion, this contrary motion helping to give the 'sense of a continually widening vista'.[4] Furthermore, in the 'Requiem æternam' tonal procedures were static, rooted to the tonic (minor and major) in the A sections, with a tonal digression in the B section reached not by argument but by juxtaposition. The repetition of the antiphon could therefore be exact, without tonal adjustments; it represents a return to the starting-point, rather than a step forward or a synthesis. For all these reasons, the 'Requiem æternam' sounds introductory, an anacrusis leading to this moment.

Tovey's words are worth recalling: '. . . the solo voices enter with the "Kyrie", which is worked out in the most moving passage in all Verdi's works; unquestionably one of the greater monuments of musical pathos'[5] (see Ex. 3.1a). The pathos is due in part to the shape of the melodic line, which arches up a seventh to the leading tone, but then falls back rather than ascending to the octave. Tonal procedures also play an important part: rather than remaining in the tonic, the tenor immediately pushes onward to the dominant, and the bass moves further afield, to the submediant. The chorus joins in after the last soloist enters, reaching a forceful cadence in the dominant (b. 96). Although the next section returns immediately to the tonic, Verdi moves away quickly, touching upon III and VI (rather than the iii and vi 'expected' in the major mode), and restoring the tonic only about thirty bars later (at b. 123 and, more definitively, at b. 130). This tonal striving is in sharp contrast to the 'Requiem æternam'.

The sudden flowering of the opening tenor solo might lead listeners to expect an operatic *largo concertato*, but Verdi soon disabuses them. What operatic quartet begins with a solo of a mere five bars, followed by the entrance

Ex. 3.1 *Requiem e Kyrie*

(a) bb. 78–82

(b) bb. 97–8

(c) bb. 101–2[6]

(d) bb. 109–11

of the three remaining singers in turn, each with similar or identical text and music? That the soloists and chorus share the same musical material is a corollary of the virtual identity of text and total lack of conflicting emotions. And note too the economy of material and consequent emphasis on techniques of variation and transformation. Virtually all of the material in the movement is drawn from the opening tenor melody and from the instrumental countermelody. After the four soloists enter with the melody first enunciated by the tenor, the full five-bar phrase never reappears, only shorter, more flexible motives derived from it – as we shall see, this is typical of Verdi's fugues as well.

The instrumental countermelody, a major-mode diminution of the descending tetrachord motive of the 'Requiem æternam' theme, not only articulates the opening of three of the sections, but also gives rise to a vocal motive that will gain importance in the course of the movement. The motive, bracketed in Ex. 3.1d, is also present in bb. 94, 98–105, 110–17 (note the augmentation in 115–17), 123–5, and 125–7 (with an expressive appoggiatura).

Furthermore, the structure of the 'Kyrie' has little to do with an operatic ensemble. The opening subsection, described above, provides a model for most of the remainder of this movement, which can usefully be divided into five subsections, or processes: (1) bb. 78–96; (2) bb. 97–108; (3) bb. 109–23; (4) bb. 123–30; (5) bb. 130–40. Each of the first four subsections begins with a point of imitation based on the principal theme – only the first and third are accompanied by the orchestral countermelody as well – building to a tutti with *forte* dynamic level and a cadence. We hear the last of the principal theme in the fourth section, where at the climax of the movement (bb. 125–30) it is overpowered by the descending fourth motive. The fifth and final subsection is dominated by the orchestral countermelody, which has proved to have a life of its own. A statement of this descending countermelody leads to a harmonic epigram, a common occurrence in Verdi's sacred works:

Ex. 3.2   *Requiem e Kyrie*: bb. 132–7 (reduction)

Then an inverted form of the countermelody – its proximity to the regular form seven bars earlier ensures that we recognize its provenance – ascends from the violas and cellos to the violins, the highest notes in the movement (save for a few notes in the piccolo).

4

Dies iræ

Dies iræ: A quattro voci (Soprano, Mezzo-Soprano, Tenore e Basso) e Coro. Beginning in G minor, ending in B♭ minor/major; 701 bars (*c.* 32–3′)

The text

The text of the Sequence 'Dies iræ', thought to have grown out of a rhymed trope to the Responsory 'Libera me', is attributed to Thomas of Celano (d. *c.* 1250). The original poem consists of eighteen rhymed stanzas: seventeen tercets and a final quatrain, the final unrhymed and unmetrical pair of lines being a later addition.[1] Like the 'Stabat mater dolorosa', another celebrated thirteenth-century Sequence often set to music, the text begins with an emotional, indeed near-hysterical, description of the scene, written in the third person. It is not until the seventh stanza ('Quid sum miser') – the book open, the judge seated – that the speaker emerges, using first person and the vocative case and imperative mood. In the final quatrain (beginning 'Lacrymosa dies illa'), vocative case and imperative mood continue, and, although there is a shift back to third person, in the fourth line ('Huic ergo parce Deus') the poet probably meant 'huic' as a self-dramatizing reference to the speaker himself, not to another 'hominem reum'. That is, there is no reason to suppose that the poet intended a shift of persona: throughout the poem it is the terrified sinner who speaks, although at the beginning and ending of the poem he retreats into the third person for rhetorical effect. As for the final couplet, it was obviously added for doctrinal rather than aesthetic reasons: it undercuts the penitential tone of the entire poem, inexplicably redirecting the plea for the speaker's own salvation, to the salvation of others ('Dona *eis* requiem').

However, whatever the medieval poet might have meant and his contemporary audience might have understood, Verdi seems to have read the poem in a more complex, equally valid manner: the first six stanzas are spoken by a narrator, albeit one emotionally caught up in the scene described. In the *Requiem* these stanzas are allotted to the chorus, except for the transitional 'Mors stupebit' and (in the definitive 1875 version only) the 'Liber scriptus'. In the seventh stanza ('Quid sum miser') the voice of the narrator yields to that of a fearful sinner who pleads for his own salvation (the tone comes perilously close to 'let everyone else be damned'). And the arrival of this new persona is signalled by an extra-liturgical reprise of the first stanza of text and some of its music – what we may call the 'Dies iræ music' – and the return of the opening key of G minor, finally nailed down with an authentic cadence at the beginning of the 'Quid sum miser'. Appropriately, these central sections are allotted almost without exception to the soloists, who speak as individuals.

Verdi places another reprise of the 'Dies iræ music' immediately before the 'Lacrymosa dies illa', significantly the stanza in which, in this reading, the narrator returns, but now pleading for mercy on behalf of both the speaker in the middle stanzas ('huic') and – because of the later, added couplet (of whose history Verdi was surely ignorant) – the entire class of sinners or endangered mortals ('eis'). In this reading of the poem, the shift to the third person in this stanza is more than a shift of tone, a rhetorical use of the third person to refer to the speaker: it marks an actual change of speaker. Verdi's draft translation of the poem suggests that this is also his interpretation, as in the line 'Huic ergo parce Deus' he incorrectly renders 'huic' as the third person *plural* 'loro', removing any possibility of self-reference: 'Perdono [date] loro, o Dio.' The 'Lacrymosa' is set as a quartet with chorus, perhaps a synthesis of the narrative voice and the voices of the individual penitents. And so both the reprises of the 'Dies iræ music' and the choice of vocal forces generally support this hypothesis about Verdi's reading of the poem.

The text of the *Dies iræ*, unlike the remaining texts in the *Requiem*, is in verse, but the structure of the poetry is significantly different from the poetry Verdi set in his operas. In the *Dies iræ* the stanzas consist of a tercet rather than the quatrain normally found in librettos, and the metre – acatalectic trochaic tetrameter with its rigidly fixed accents on every other syllable ($- \cup - \cup - \cup - \cup$) – is less flexible even than the Italian *ottonario* metre that it resembles. Had Verdi had a librettist in tow he would have insisted that each stanza end with a '*verso tronco*': that the line should end with an accented syllable, facilitating a strong cadence on the downbeat. Throughout the *Dies iræ* Verdi needed to find ways of providing these cadences while avoiding faulty declamation. His usual solution is to lengthen the penultimate, stressed syllable and to limit the final, unstressed syllable to a relatively short value.

The reprises

All three reprises of the 'Dies iræ music' – two within the *Dies iræ* and a final one in the *Libera me* – are drawn from the opening sixty-one bars of the movement. They follow the initial presentation of the music exactly, so that in Verdi's autograph only the first presentation is written out in full: cues direct the copyists back to the opening of the *Dies iræ* for the complete orchestration.[2] There are of course precedents for recurring *music* in *Dies iræ* settings – for example, in Cherubini's C–minor Requiem, the Requiems of Paisiello and Donizetti, and, for that matter, in the strophic structure of the plainchant itself. However, Verdi's extra-liturgical reprises of text as well as music are unusual, perhaps even unique. Like the other two extra-liturgical reprises of text in the *Requiem* – in the *Lux æterna* and in the *Offertorio* – the two reprises of the 'Dies iræ' text within the *Dies iræ* movement are linked to a reprise of the music associated with that text.[3] Verdi may have introduced these textual reprises primarily to 'justify' musical reprises wanted on independent grounds – as though he were reluctant to provide a large-scale musical reprise without the original text.[4] In the *Dies iræ* the reprises articulate the changes in voice from the narrator to the 'characters', as well as helping to bind together into a single number the movement's many (ten) sections.

'Dies iræ'

'Dies iræ': Coro – bb. 1–90. Orchestra: tutti. G minor (ending ambiguously); Allegro agitato, $\mathbf{C}$ ($\downarrow = 80$); 90 bars (*c.* 2'15")

Dies iræ, dies illa	Day of wrath, that day
Solvet sæclum in favilla,	will dissolve the generations into ashes –
Teste David cum Sibylla.	so say David and Sibyl, the prophetess.
Quantus tremor est futurus,	How great a trembling there shall be
Quando Judex est venturus,	when the Judge shall come
Cuncta stricte discussurus!	and separate everything strictly.

Fig. 4.1 'Dies iræ' text

One could hardly improve upon Julian Budden's description of the opening: 'conceived as an unearthly storm: four tutti thunderclaps, later separated by powerful blows on the bass drum, the skin tightened to give a hard dry sound (the Shakespearean "crack of doom"?); rapid scales in contrary motion:

peremptory calls to attention on the brass, and a chromatic choral line collapsing into those slow triplets that Verdi will use again for the real storm in *Otello*.[5] The force of this outburst is 'intensified by the tonal non sequitur (A major – G minor)'. Much of the music setting the first stanza was originally drafted for the 1869 *Libera me* and might best be examined in the discussion of that revision (pp. 64–7).

In the second stanza (beginning 'Quantus tremor'), the theme is transformed into a quiet staccato 'clockwork' version, reminiscent of the transformations of the opening strains of the third movement of Beethoven's Fifth Symphony. The transformed theme is accompanied by several topoi associated with terror, grace-note lament figures in the winds, 'shuddering strings', and in the timpani the anapestic figures that are frequently – but by no means invariably – associated with death.[6] In the first line the chorus depicts 'tremor' literally, with long pauses separating words and even syllables. This 'stammering topos', as we may call it, appears with some frequency in the *Requiem*. For the second and third lines, the chorus shifts to a solemn, 'oracular' declamation on repeated notes, with an exaggerated differentiation between the length of accented and unaccented syllables, an obsessive repetition of the same rhythmic pattern, and an extremely slow delivery of the text – a cross between the Commendatore in the second finale of *Don Giovanni* and Zaccaria's opening lines in *Nabucco*. As in Verdi's ritual scenes, all this unfolds in a threefold sequence, here ascending from E♭ minor, through F minor, to G minor (the last statement cut off by an unexpected C-minor chord).

'Tuba mirum'

'Tuba mirum': Coro – bb. 91–139. Orchestra: tutti, plus 4 off-stage trumpets. A♭ minor (ending with V/d); Allegro sostenuto (then animando a poco a poco in the last 35 bars); ₵ (initial tempo: ♩ = 88); 49 bars (*c*. 2'–2'15")

Tuba mirum spargens sonum	The trumpet, throwing its wondrous sound
Per sepulchra regionum,	through the tombs of the earth
Coget omnes ante thronum.	will summon all before the throne.

Fig. 4.2 'Tuba mirum' text

Part of a critic's task in the nineteenth century – a period in which 'originality' was prized – was to detect and pillory musical borrowings, and Ernest Reyer devotes almost a quarter of his highly favourable review to Verdi's supposed indebtedness to the 'Tuba mirum' of Berlioz's *Grande messe des morts*, a passage Verdi probably knew, if only from the excerpt published in Berlioz's treatise on instrumentation (see p. 9).[7] There are indeed similarities between the two works: the antiphonal treatment (but with a mere two pairs of off-stage trumpets rather than Berlioz's 'quatre petits Orchestres d'instruments de cuivre'), the repeated notes in anapestic rhythm (the relationship is especially clear at the outset of the two movements) and triplet fanfares, the prominence of E♭ major (but as tonic in Berlioz, and dominant in Verdi) with the intrusion of a disturbing D♭, and, after about two dozen bars of orchestral music, the entrance of the choral basses in their high register. But rather than starting out *fortissimo* on the tonic, Verdi starts quietly (*mezzo forte* but dropping to *piano*) with a single note on the dominant, gradually adding intensity by increasing volume, adding instruments, speeding up the tempo ('animando a poco a poco') and level of rhythmic activity. All this is a prolongation of the dominant, leading to a powerful cadence in A♭ minor, the local tonic (b. 111). The two composers seem to have striven for – or at least they achieved – very different effects. Berlioz's 'Tuba mirum', rather like his 'Rex tremendæ', suggests awe, but not fear; in both cases Verdi evokes terror. Verdi's piece is abruptly cut off with a shriek by the entire chorus and orchestra on an unexpected A-major chord, functioning here as the Neapolitan chord of A♭ minor, but immediately reinterpreted as V/d in the following section.

'Mors stupebit'

'Mors stupebit': Solo per Basso – bb. 140–61. Orchestra: woodwinds (minus flute and piccolo), horns, bass drum, and strings. V/d; Molto meno mosso; 𝄵 (♩ = 72); 22 bars (*c*. 1'15")

Mors stupebit et natura	Death and nature will stand stupefied
Cum resurget creatura,	when those dead arise
Judicanti responsura.	to answer Him who judges.

Fig. 4.3 'Mors stupebit' text

The entire 'Mors stupebit' prolongs the A-major chord that ended the 'Tuba mirum', and in a quiet but insistent way – note the pedal A[1] in the basses, doubled by the bass drum – it provides very strong dominant preparation for a cadence in D minor. The bass soloist both acts out and, in the persona of a narrator, describes the amazement of Death. Verdi uses both of the declamatory topoi found in the 'Quantus tremor' stanza: the stammering topos is especially evident in the final chromatic descent with its threefold utterance of 'Mors'. (It is also found in Cherubini's two Requiems, especially in the C-minor one, and in Berlioz's work, though in different musical dialects.) Of this passage Verdi wrote '[There is] nothing easier than, for example, those four notes of the bass [on] "Mors stupebit" but [they are] so difficult to perform well!'[8]

'Liber scriptus'

'Liber scriptus' (definitive version):[9] Solo per Mezzo-Soprano (including transition into reprise) – bb. 162–238. Orchestra: tutti, minus piccolo and bass drum. D minor; Allegro molto sostenuto, $\mathbf{C}$ ($\downarrow$ = 88; $\downarrow$ = 80 in the last 3 bars); 77 bars (3'30")

Original version: Coro – Fuga (bb. 162a–215a). Orchestra: woodwinds (minus piccolo, horns and trumpets) and strings. G minor; Allegro assai mosso, $\mathbf{C}$ ($\downarrow$ = 144); 54 bars (1'30")

Liber scriptus proferetur,	The written record shall be brought forth
In quo totum continetur,	wherein all is contained
Unde mundus judicetur.	by which the world is judged.
Judex ergo cum sedebit,	When the Judge, therefore, shall preside,
Quidquid latet apparebit,	anything concealed shall appear,
Nil inultum remanebit.	nothing shall remain unpunished.

Fig. 4.4 'Liber scriptus' text

The revised 'Liber scriptus' is the first extended solo in the *Requiem*, and its text is of course in verse rather than prose: it is in such numbers – the solos and small ensembles in the *Dies iræ* – that we might expect to find Verdi having recourse to musical shapes resembling those in his operas. In his early and middle-period operas, he had a standard procedure for setting the initial presentation of a double quatrain of text (i.e., two four-line stanzas), a 'lyric prototype' of about sixteen bars, in which each line of text takes up two bars. After a thematic block of two matching phrases (a_4 a'_4 or a_4 a_4), there is contrasting material (b_4), often arranged as a pair of two-bar phrases, providing a sense of acceleration (b_2 b'_2).[10] The final pair of lines is set either as a return to the initial idea (a''_4), or as a new, often climactic phrase (c_4). Such structures can still be found in *Aida*, but by this time Verdi had other favoured phrase structures as well. The four-phrase lyric prototype appears unmodified but once in the *Requiem*, but has resonances elsewhere, especially in the *Dies iræ*.

The opening of the 'Liber scriptus' continues to prolong V/d, as the mezzo-soprano, at first seemingly unable to move beyond the doggedly repeated a¹s and the fifth above,[11] frees herself with an imposing eight-bar phrase ending with a forceful cadence in D minor, finally resolving the dominant that has been sounding since the last chord of the 'Tuba mirum'. The chorus closes off the stanza with a murmured 'Dies iræ' (b. 177). Although the stanza is only three lines long, through text repetition Verdi expands the paragraph to sixteen bars, the same length as the lyric prototype (setting eight lines). Here the phrase structure might be expressed as $a_4\ a'_4\ c_8$ (showing the presence of a final cadential phrase but the lack of the usual medial phrase or phrases).

The setting of the second stanza resembles the lyric prototype: the thematic block $d_4\ d'_5$ is followed by $e_2\ e'_2$, although the second phrase (bb. 194–5) elides into a three-bar extension based on the sequential descending thirds from c (compare bb. 171–4 and bb. 195–7). The final phrase consists of familiar material, not d, but c, the eight-bar descending phrase that concluded the *first* stanza. This linking of large paragraphs by a recurring phrase is found in the 'Quid sum miser', 'Recordare', and 'Ingemisco' as well.

At this point the text has been exhausted, but Verdi repeats it in the last third of this expansive piece. The first stanza (bb. 206–13) is declaimed over a tonic pedal and a repeated phrase in the orchestra. The third presentation builds to an explosion on a diminished-seventh chord – a radical reharmonization of that tonic pedal – with the mezzo-soprano reaching a♭², her highest note in the *Requiem*. The chorus again intones 'Dies iræ', still on D, but now without the effect of closure that obtained before (in bb. 177 and 191).

On the repetition of the second stanza (bb. 214ff.) the mezzo-soprano declaims on a dotted rhythm the first two lines on d¹, which functions as a pedal, the orchestra sliding downward with different harmonizations of it. As she stammers the final line, the harmony spins through a remarkable modulating circle of fifths (from V⁷/A♭ to V⁷/d, the return thwarted by a deceptive cadence), followed by a rhetorical pause and a *fortissimo* outburst on a dissonant iv⁷ chord, her line both recalling her earlier cadential phrase and looking forward to other emphatic closing gestures given to mezzo-soprano and soprano soloists in the *Requiem*.[12]

When music imitates a speaker who stammers because of the burden of emotion, weeps with stylized sobs, or prays in an imitation of plainchant, it can be said to accomplish a 'performative act' and can force the reading that, despite the literal sense of the text, the singer is – or might as well be – a character, rather than an abstract, narrative voice.[13] That is the case here, where, although the text remains in the third person, the mezzo-soprano speaks as a character.

The ominous background activity at the end of the solo (bb. 229ff.), the sequential descending thirds (now separated by two bars), and the chorus's muttered 'Dies iræ' provide a transition to the first of three reprises of the 'Dies iræ music'.[14] The transition is necessary because this reprise, unlike the others, begins not with the opening but *in medias res*, with the dissonant chord (g: V_7^9/iv) that forms the climax of the section.

Reprise of the 'Dies iræ music' (bb. 239–69, including a literal reprise of *Dies iræ*, bb. 46–60; *c*. 45"). This leads to V^7/g, but the expected cadence is interrupted by silence.

'Quid sum miser'

'Quid sum miser': A tre voci (Soprano, Mezzo-Soprano e Tenore) – bb. 270–321. Orchestra: flutes, oboes, clarinets, bassoon 1, horn 3, strings. G minor; Adagio, $\frac{6}{8}$ (♪ = 100); 52 bars (3'00"–3'15")

Quid sum miser tunc dicturus,	What am I to say then, wretch that I am?
Quem patronum rogaturus,	Whom shall I call as patron
Cum vix justus sit securus?	when scarcely the just may be secure?

Fig. 4.5 'Quid sum miser' text

The 'Quid sum miser' opens with a closing, cadential figure in the clarinets – a disturbingly anticlimactic resolution after the strong dominant preparation – and a figure in the solo bassoon that repeats obsessively for much of the piece. The prominent soloistic use of the winds and the reintroduction of vocal soloists mark the emergence of the individual penitents, who now speak in the first person singular. After the cadence ending the mezzo-soprano's first phrase, the process repeats: the clarinets and bassoon restate their opening material, and the singer presents the second line to the same melody. Rather than closing as before, however, she anxiously lurches forward into the final line ('Cum vix justus sit securus?'), set to a desperate descending gesture. Her melody ends on $\hat{5}$ rather than cadencing to $\hat{1}$ (perhaps reflecting the question mark in the text), and the clarinets' cadential figure returns one bar earlier than expected, superimposed upon the dominant (and thus enriched with a pungent augmented triad at b. 283). The soloist's rushing into her concluding phrase and the 'premature' entrance of the clarinets is emblematic of the 'Quid sum miser', in which both the space separating the later paragraphs and the paragraphs themselves are compressed.

The second paragraph (bb. 285ff.) begins similarly to the first, but after the tenor's first phrase, the soprano and mezzo-soprano enter two bars early. An attempt to modulate to III (B♭ major) is thwarted and the descending gesture, followed by the cadential figure, inexorably returns. The third paragraph (bb. 296ff.) begins with the three soloists unaccompanied and starting out optimistically with new material in III, but the orchestra (most notably the bassoon) re-enters, forcing them back to G minor and the last appearance of the desperate refrain and the cadential figure. The fourth paragraph (b. 304), beginning after a mere eighth rest, employs the stammering topos again: the first three words are set to sobbing appoggiaturas – elsewhere Verdi often labels such motives 'lamento' – and separated by silence.[15] A more lyrical phrase shifts to the tonic major, and on its repetition Verdi adds an additional bar allowing the soprano's line to arch up to b♮^{2} – 'dolce' is the usually neglected indication.

In the coda (bb. 314ff.) the lamento motive reappears, now intensified into a semitone (a♭–g). The consolatory turn from G minor to the parallel major proves to be illusory, as the latter is reinterpreted as a harsh dominant-ninth chord of C minor. The unaccompanied phrases of the three soloists that conclude this section prolong this dissonant chord, the soprano's final question brusquely answered by the *fortissimo* cadence that initiates the 'Rex tremendæ majestatis'. Because of the unresolved conflict between G minor and C minor for control of the 'Dies iræ music' (see pp. 64–5), the first authentic cadence in G minor in the entire *Requiem* occurs only at the onset of the 'Quid sum miser'; but, because of this reinterpretation of G as V/c, the ambiguity continues.

'Rex tremendæ majestatis'

'Rex tremendæ majestatis': A quattro voci (Soprano, Mezzo-Soprano, Tenore e Basso) e Coro – bb. 322–82. Orchestra: tutti. C minor (ending in C major); Adagio maestoso, **C** ($\rfloor$ = 72); 61 bars (3'15")

Rex tremendæ majestatis,	King of great majesty
Qui salvandos salvas gratis,	Who by Grace save those so destined,
Salva me, fons pietatis.	save me, fountain of mercy.

Fig. 4.6 'Rex tremendæ majestatis' text

The 'Rex tremendæ majestatis' section is unique in the central portion of the *Dies iræ* – the part of the text spoken by the terrified sinner, not the narrator – for its use of chorus in addition to the soloists. The text consists of a single stanza, two lines apostrophizing the King, followed by a plea for mercy in the third line. If this were an opera, the composer would doubtless have set the entire stanza as the speech of a single character who addresses the King and then begs for salvation. But considerations of verisimilitude would have dictated an abject, terrified setting of the opening line, a setting of humble awe, rather than a powerful one that captured the sense of tremendous, fear-inspiring majesty, of *terribilità*. As in the corresponding sections of the Requiems of Mozart and Cherubini, Verdi contrasts a violent setting of the opening lines with a quiet, lyrical setting of the final plea, the response suggested by the text. But unlike the earlier works, which use the chorus throughout the section, Verdi also effects a shift from a narrative voice portraying the concept 'Rex tremendæ majestatis' – the chorus – to the voices of the individual penitents portrayed by the soloists.

The section can usefully be divided into five stages. In the first (bb. 322–35), Verdi set the 'Rex tremendæ majestatis' image as a jagged line spanning a twelfth in double-dotted rhythms, sung by the choral basses. By using dotted rhythms in a slow tempo here, Verdi, like Mozart, Cherubini (in the D-minor Requiem), and Berlioz in their 'Rex tremendæ' movements, adopts a time-honoured topos for evoking the majesty of the celestial and/ or earthly Lord (e.g. Louis XIV).[16] Significantly, Verdi, like Cherubini (again in the D-minor work) and Berlioz, included 'maestoso' in his tempo indication. The soloists then beg for mercy – 'Salva me' – on a lyrical, major-mode transformation of the first five notes of the opening idea: the dotted rhythms are smoothed out and the range of the melody is reduced to a major sixth by means of octave displacement of the first note (compare Ex. 4.1a and b).

Despite their surface lyricism, these pleas are unsettled and urgent. Each statement appears over a (local) dominant pedal, so the effect is V^{6-7}_{4-3} on each step, the vocal line left hanging on $\hat{2}$. Furthermore, the three pleas are dissociated tonally, as each is transposed a minor third higher in a modulating sequence. After this attempt to escape, the soloists are pulled back harshly by the re-entrance of the choral basses with a *fortissimo* statement of the 'Rex tremendæ' motive in its original shape, momentarily in the tonic major (as V/iv).[17] The passage therefore arpeggiates a diminished-seventh chord on C (c–e♭–g♭–a): this chord will assume greater significance later.

Verdi has thus set up a conflict between two contrasting (though related) motives. In the first stage they are presented separately, while in the second

Ex. 4.1 'Rex tremendæ majestatis'

(a) bb. 322–5 (of *Dies iræ*)

(b) bb. 330–1

they appear in intense, close alternation. Then they are separated once again, with each of the final three stages governed by one of the motives, the other motive absent. Throughout the piece, the menacing 'Rex tremendæ majestatis' motive remains primarily the domain of the choral basses; the more lyrical 'Salva me' motive and its transformations, primarily that of the soloists, especially the three upper voices. But there is no consistent mapping of performing forces, text, and musical material. With one exception (the choral tenors' hushed replies near the opening), the three upper voices – of soloists and chorus alike – are restricted to the third line of text (though not invariably sung to the 'Salva me' motive); however, both the bass soloist and the choral basses eventually sing all three lines of text. And at one point the bass soloist, temporarily ceasing to be a 'character', allies himself with the narrative voice conveyed by the chorus. Unlike the situation in opera, a given singer may shift roles rapidly, now functioning as narrator, now representing a character.

In the second stage (bb. 336–46), Verdi presents the two ideas in close alternation. Ex. 4.2a shows the transformations of the 'Salva me' motive. While this motive undergoes frequent transformations, that associated with 'Rex tremendæ' appears in more or less its original shape. Ex. 4.2b shows its only transformation in the entire piece (bb. 342–5).

The second stage ends upon the same diminished-seventh chord that the soloists had outlined earlier – c–e♭–g♭–a – but now heard as a thwarted pre-dominant of E♭ minor.

Ex. 4.2 'Rex tremendæ majestatis'

(a) Soprano part, bb. 337–42

(b) Bass solo and strings, bb. 342–5

The calmer third stage (bb. 347–56) is based on further transformations of the 'Salva me' motive (see Ex. 4.3); neither the 'Rex tremendæ' text nor its motive appear.

This stage begins in the tonally remote region of F♯ major (suggested by the ⁶₄ chord in that key but never confirmed by a cadence) then gradually makes its way back to C minor, its cadence foreshadowing the head of the fugue subject of the *Libera me*. This is the first authentic cadence in any key in the 'Rex tremendæ', and it is relatively weak because of its reduced scoring, quiet dynamic level, and the understated dominant preparation: a mere two beats.

In the fourth stage (bb. 356–69) the conflict between the 'Rex tremendæ' and 'Salva me' is resolved – or nearly so. The choral basses again assert the

Ex. 4.3 'Rex tremendæ majestatis': Soloists, bb. 346–54

'Rex tremendæ' motive, the bass soloist echoing their text and dotted rhythm, but to a different figure. The remaining soloists and chorus repeat 'Salva me', but, significantly, set not to the familiar lyrical theme, but to a new unrelated figure. In the course of this stage the dotted-rhythm motive (and its semantic baggage), the first two lines of text, and the narrator's terrifying voice are definitively abandoned, or, one might say, vanquished. The soprano carries her line to c^3 and at the cadence turns to major. Note too that in the course of the cadence the prominent diminished-seventh chord – now heard and spelled as a pre-dominant of C minor (c–e♭–f♯– a) – finally resolves (bb. 366–8). This is a far stronger cadence than the only previous authentic cadence, but nonetheless the soprano and tenor end on 3̂ rather than 1̂.

But there is other unfinished business to be attended to as well: the 'Salva me' theme still has not been heard in a tonally stable statement. After the cadence, the bass soloist tentatively proposes its first three notes, but neutralized rhythmically and augmented to half-notes (Ex. 4.4a). The chorus

Ex. 4.4   'Rex tremendæ majestatis'

(a)   bb. 370–1

(b)   bb. 376–9

takes this up eagerly, accelerating to quarter-notes. Each entrance begins a third above its predecessor, so when the motive finally reaches the solo soprano and tenor on the eighth entrance it has returned to its starting-point, C. This is of course a stabilized re-enactment of the first presentation of the lyrical theme, there too begun by the bass soloist (at bb. 330–1). But in that earlier presentation the passage was a modulating sequence moving by minor thirds, while here it is a tonal sequence remaining within C major. At first the soprano and tenor seem to accept the motive as though it were simply another step in the sequence, but then they transform it, making the three-note motive blossom out into a broad lyrical statement of the 'Salva me' theme (Ex. 4.4b). This gesture – passing a motive up to the highest voices, who then expand and transform it – seems inseparably bound to vocal sonority: in a piano piece, for example, it would be far less effective.[18]

As noted earlier, the first presentations of the 'Salva me' theme were left suspended on $\hat{2}$. So the soprano and tenor here finally provide closure, presenting this theme – and by extension the 'Rex tremendæ' theme from which it is derived – as a four-bar phrase in the tonic key, which we may allow ourselves to hear as its 'real' form, the form towards which both themes had been striving all along. This is an important moment: it is the strongest closure heard thus far in the *Dies iræ*, and, according to Verdi's metronome indications, it falls almost exactly at the halfway point of the movement. Note too that after the choral sections at the beginning of the *Dies iræ*, the sections with soloists have traced an upward path, with solos for bass and mezzo-soprano followed by a trio for the three highest voices, leading to the 'Rex tremendæ,' a climactic quartet with chorus. With the 'Recordare' the trajectory reverses itself, with a duet for the two women, solos for tenor then bass, leading to the concluding quartet with chorus, the 'Lacrymosa'.[19]

In the struggle between the jagged 'Rex tremendæ majestatis' melodic line and its lyrical transformation ('Salva me') the latter has won, neutralizing the threat inherent in the former. Had the *Requiem* ended here, the supplicants might well have been optimistic about the reception of their plea for mercy.

George Bernard Shaw quipped, 'Certainly, where you come to a strong Italian like Verdi you may be quite sure that if you cannot explain him without dragging in the great Germans, you cannot explain him at all.'[20] Nonetheless, it should be observed that Verdi's procedure in this section is similar to one found in music of the high Classical period, especially that of Beethoven: thematic material is initially problematized – either by a destabilizing element within the theme itself (whether chromaticism, irregular phrase structure, or other means) or by its appearance in a tonal area that challenges the tonic – and eventually a stabilized reprise of that thematic material provides resolution, in a way that an equally stable presentation of *new* thematic material could not.[21] We shall see other examples of this procedure, where reprise serves as resolution, in the *Offertorio* and *Lux æterna*, and at least an analogous strategy in the *Sanctus* and *Libera me* fugues.

After the final cadence, a three-note motive sets up the accompaniment figure that will permeate the following section (which adopts the 'stesso tempo').

'Recordare'

'Recordare': A due voci (Soprano e Mezzo-Soprano) – bb. 383–446. Orchestra: woodwinds (minus piccolo), horns, strings. F major; Stesso tempo (i.e., Adagio maestoso, ♩ = 72), but 'animando sempre' later; **C**; 64 bars (*c.* 3'15"–3'30")

Recordare Jesu pie,	Remember, merciful Jesus,
Quod sum causa tuæ viæ	that I am the cause of Thy journey.
Ne me perdas illa die.	Do not destroy me on that day.
Quærens me, sedisti lassus,	Seeking me, Thou didst sit weary;
Redimisti crucem passus:	Thou didst redeem me, having suffered the cross.
Tantus labor non sit cassus.	May so much suffering not be in vain.

Juste Judex ultionis,	As the just Judge of vengeance
Donum fac remissionis	grant the gift of remission
Ante diem rationis.	before the day of reckoning.

Fig. 4.7 'Recordare' text

In the 'Recordare', the supplicant has found reason to hope for salvation, and leaves off his confessions of guilt, turning from the 'King of great majesty' to 'merciful Jesus': the opening is one of the most serene passages in the movement, as is the corresponding section in Mozart's *Dies iræ*. The first two lines, sung first by the mezzo-soprano and repeated (with a slight expansion) by the soprano, are treated with utmost calm, over a rocking figure in the cello and a static tonic pedal, while the high woodwinds recall the 'Salva me' invocation from stage 3 of the 'Rex tremendæ'. The final line of the stanza, with its reminder that perdition remains a possibility, turns to the tonic minor but concludes in the major, the voices finally joining together.

The second stanza, with its tale of Jesus's suffering, turns again to the minor mode, with the two soloists frequently singing sobbing figures in parallel thirds: a texture found more often in opera than in the *Requiem*. The third stanza, like the first, is a plea for mercy, without the breast-beating of the 'Quid sum miser' or the 'Ingemisco', and it is appropriately set to a reprise of the opening, major-mode music. However, this reprise is interrupted by the deceptive cadence at b. 429. The operatic cadenza at bb. 434–8 adds generic expectations for a strong cadence, so the second deceptive cadence at b. 439 is even more disruptive than the first. The expected authentic cadence is avoided until the very end of the 'Recordare'; in conjunction with the 'animando sempre fino alla fine' this results in considerable tension.

It is worth noting that the music of the second and third stanzas, with its a_4 a'_4 b_2 b'_2 c_8 phrase structure, is similar to the 'lyric prototype', with three important qualifications: c (the third stanza) is not new material, but a reprise of music from the first stanza; it is twice as long as the usual c_4; and it is followed by an unusually spacious continuation.

'Ingemisco'

'Ingemisco': Solo per Tenore – bb. 447–502. Orchestra: woodwinds, horns, and strings. E♭ major; no change of tempo until the 'Poco meno mosso' at b. 457, **C**; 56 bars (3'15"–3'30")

Ingemisco tamquam reus:	I groan like a criminal;
Culpa rubet vultus meus:	blame reddens my face.
Supplicanti parce Deus.	God, spare a supplicant.
Qui Mariam absolvisti,	Thou who didst absolve Mary [Magdalene]
Et latronem exaudisti,	and accepted the robber's plea,
Mihi quoque spem dedisti.	to me, as well, Thou gavest hope.
Preces meæ non sunt dignæ,	My prayers are not worthy,
Sed tu bonus fac benigne,	but, Kind One, grant
Ne perenni cremer igne.	that I may not burn in eternal fire.
Inter oves locum præsta,	Give me place among the sheep,
Et ab hædis me sequestra,	separate me from the goats,
Statuens in parte dextra.	placing me by Thy right hand.

Fig. 4.8 'Ingemisco' text

The text of this section consists of four stanzas, more than that of any other section of the *Dies iræ*. Verdi solves the potential problem of excessive length by setting the first and third stanzas, with their self-deprecation, in a declamatory fashion, the calmer, more optimistic second and fourth stanzas as more expansive lyrical statements. Nonetheless, all four stanzas are linked through motivic connections (see Ex. 4.5).

The first stanza is set as an arioso, with syllabic declamation and almost no text repetition. The first two lines, set in C minor, dwell upon the supplicant's guilt; the plea of the third line turns to C major, setting off the main tonality of E♭ major more strikingly than C minor would have done. In the second stanza he finds reason to hope, and the tenor has broad, lyrical phrases, marked *dolce con calma*. As in the 'Recordare' there are resonances of the lyric prototype. The stanza opens with the $a_4 a'_4$ thematic block (note that the vocal line is identical in both statements, but harmonized differently) but continues with $b_1 b'_1 c_4$, ending in V rather than I. The return to the tonic, which occurs only later, is a special moment.

The third stanza returns to the speaker's realization of his unworthiness then shifts to a plea that he be spared the unpleasantness of eternal fire. Although a plea for the avoidance of negative consequences is logically equivalent to a plea for a positive good – e.g., being placed at God's right hand, as in the final stanza – composers will naturally treat them differently. The third stanza, especially its first line, is set in a declamatory style over ostinato-like statements derived from the triplet figure of the opening bar of the second stanza. For the first two lines the speaker obsessively repeats the alternating

Ex. 4.5 'Ingemisco'

(a) bb. 447–52

(b) bb. 457–60

(c) bb. 470–2

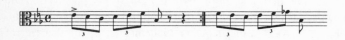

(d) bb. 478–80

c♭ and b♭, which lend a minor-mode colouring. The final stanza returns to a lyrical setting, with a melody closely related to that of the second stanza; indeed, it begins with an exact inversion of the first bar of the second stanza ('Qui Mariam').[22] This appears in the dominant (B♭ major), and the tenor echoes the last two bars of the theme (bb. 482–4) in the parallel minor, provoking a move further afield to ♭III (G♭ major). The threatened cadence there is evaded (bb. 487–8), giving way to a triumphant five-bar statement of the 'Qui Mariam' melody, and it is in the course of this phrase that the return to I (E♭) is achieved and stabilized with a cadence. And so, as in the 'Liber scriptus', 'Quid sum miser', and 'Recordare', a phrase from the initial paragraph of the section returns to round off structures far broader than the norm in opera. Here the effect is especially powerful as the thematic return is perceived as having brought about the tonal return. The movement closes with statements of the first two bars of the 'Inter oves' – the quasi-ostinato treatment here foreshadows that at the end of the 'Hostias' – and, under the tenor's b♭[1], a final hint of the opening of the 'Qui Mariam' theme.

Not surprisingly, even from the beginning commentators connected the 'Ingemisco' with opera. Filippo Filippi, Italy's foremost music critic at the time, placed it within the 'genere drammatico', noting that there were even the 'obligatory triplets', while both Reyer and Hanslick were reminded of *Aida*.[23]

'Confutatis maledictis'

'Confutatis maledictis': Solo per Basso – bb. 503–72. Orchestra: woodwinds, horns, timpani, and strings. E major; Andante, **C** (♩ = 96); 70 bars (3'00")

Confutatis maledictis,	When the damned are confounded
Flammis acribus addictis,	and consigned to bitter flames
Voca me cum benedictis.	call me with the blessed ones.
Oro supplex et acclinis,	I pray, supplicant and prostrate,
Cor contritum quasi cinis,	heart contrite as if in ashes
Gere curam mei finis.	have a care for my end.

Fig. 4.9 'Confutatis maledictis' text

The form of the 'Confutatis maledictis' can be expressed as A B A' C B Coda, as the letters in the margin indicate.

A As in the 'Rex tremendæ', the text of the first tercet incorporates a sharp contrast: the first two lines might again be associated with a narrative voice, the last line reverting to the voice of the supplicant.[24] The contrast is stronger in the settings of Mozart and Cherubini, for Verdi, preferring to emphasize the longer-range contrast between the two stanzas, moves through the first stanza quickly, postponing lyrical expansion of its final line for the restatement.

B Verdi's setting of the second stanza ('Oro supplex') includes the consecutive fifths (in fact, consecutive triads; bb. 512, 515) discussed by writers as diverse as Hanslick and Reyer (both objected to them, while recognizing that they were clearly intentional),[25] and Felix Salzer (who defended them by arguing that they do not belong to the basic voice-leading, but merely function as a kind of doubling).[26] For Tovey, Verdi's consecutive fifths (here and in the setting of 'omnis terra veneretur' in the *Te Deum*) express a 'negation of classical part-writing appropriate to the sentiment of utter self-abasement'. But Budden asks 'why . . . the same device [should] occur in the Consecration scene of *Aida*'. 'More probably', he suggests, 'Verdi was aiming in both cases at an antique organum-like solemnity that antedates the rules of part-writing.' But it is difficult to find a single affect common to these examples and such others as the end of Section II of the *Libera me*, the opening of the final scene of *Aida*, and the end of Act II of *Otello*.

The three lines of text are set as three statements of a three-bar phrase, as though the speaker were obsessed with his guilt. Similarly, this repetitive pattern is followed by another (bb. 519–23): a one-bar phrase is repeated twice (although the third statement is extended by an extra bar). The 'Oro supplex' stanza began in C♯ minor (vi) with this second pattern moving to E minor. It is only with the concluding four-bar cadential phrase (bb. 524–7) that the tonic E major is finally achieved. Incidentally, the 'Confutatis' and the 'Kyrie' are the only pieces in sharp keys in the entire *Requiem*.

A' Although the declamation of the first two lines is still restricted to only four bars, it is intensified with a rising sequence and a more active accompaniment (Reyer found that the scales in contrary motion and trombone [*recte* horn] blasts 'expressed in the most dramatic way the terror of the damned').[27] Unlike the A subsection, now Verdi exploits the sharp contrast between the first two lines and the third, expanding the setting of the third line into a separate section:

C in which the bass sings a lyrical line, marked 'dolce cantabile', with overlapping entries in the woodwinds.

B The 'Oro supplex' returns, with an expansion of the cadential phrase which now peaks on e¹, the bass's highest note in the *Requiem*.

Coda A new figure appears over the familiar repeated eighths of the accompaniment, turning to the tonic minor. The final plea, 'Gere curam mei finis', is answered with a violent deceptive cadence, as the bass's trill on f♯ slides up to g and the expected E-minor chord is replaced by the *fortissimo* G-minor chords that open the 'Dies iræ music'. This 'brusque transition' and the parallel fifths earlier in the 'Confutatis' were the principal 'légers défauts' cited by Reyer in his generally laudatory review. Filippi, on the other hand, praised the transition as 'highly daring' and compared it to Beethoven's putting together 'all the notes of the diatonic scale in the Ninth Symphony'.[28]

Reprise of the 'Dies iræ music' (bb. 573–623; including an exact reprise of bb. 1–26; 1'15"–1'30")

This veers into unstable diminished-seventh chords and a sudden cataclysmic shift to a *fortissimo* Eb-minor triad (iv/bb), upon which the sopranos reintroduce the familiar descending gesture, with a rapid decrescendo, leading to the final stage of the transition to the 'Lacrymosa'.

'Lacrymosa'

'Lacrymosa': A quattro voci (Soprano, Mezzo-Soprano, Tenore e Basso) e Coro – bb. 624–701. Orchestra: tutti. Bb minor (ending in Bb major); Largo, **C** ($\downarrow = 60$); 78 bars (*c.* 5'15")

Lacrymosa dies illa,	Tearful shall be that day
Qua resurget ex favilla,	when arises from the ashes
Judicandus homo reus.	evil man, to be judged.
Huic ergo parce Deus:	Therefore spare this man, God.
Pie Jesu, Domine,	Merciful Lord Jesus,
Dona eis requiem. Amen.	grant them rest. Amen.

Fig. 4.10 'Lacrymosa' text

As noted above, the principal melody of this section derives from a duet written for *Don Carlos* but suppressed during the rehearsals. (The process of revision of the theme is discussed below [see pp. 76–9]). Reyer preferred the developments of the melody to the melody itself,[29] and indeed, the 'Lacrymosa', like the two other quartets with chorus, makes extensive use of variation technique and thematic transformation.

The theme is first sung by the mezzo-soprano; when the bass restates it, she continues with a syncopated ascending counterpoint marked 'piangente', and her sobs break off each syllable. The following pair of two-bar phrases is a tonal contrast, starting immediately in III, but its motivic material is clearly drawn from the theme. This was needed to provide a momentary contrast before the main theme was presented once again, in a quiet tutti.

This third and last complete presentation of the theme is sung by the tenors and basses at the unison, with two countermelodies, one sung by the mezzo-soprano soloist and the women of the chorus, the other, again a gasping syncopated 'lamentoso' figure, by the soprano soloist, who carries her line up to bb^2 and a deceptive cadence to V^7/V (b. 653). Most of the remainder of the movement is taken up with development of the theme. In bb. 653–7 the sopranos and altos of the chorus present the first phrase of the theme, the soprano soloist simultaneously singing a free inversion. In bb. 657–61 the theme is reduced to five notes and moves through the circle of fifths from f to d♭ over a bass that descends by step through two octaves and a fourth (allowing for octave transposition, of course). The passage ends with the final phrase of the theme, counterpointing the soprano's climactic phrase, and ending with the consecutive octaves that Verdi not infrequently uses for especially decisive cadences.

The setting of 'Pie Jesu, Domine/Dona eis requiem', for the unaccompanied soloists, finally relinquishes the theme (although the cadential phrase recalls that of the opening phrase of the theme). Filippi spoke of the 'tranquille e religiose armonie'.[30] This passage begins in VI (G♭), and its first half consists entirely of a G♭ triad inflected by appoggiaturas on the strong beats. However, like the earlier attempted escape to III (bb. 641–5), it inexorably returns to B♭ minor and the principal theme.

The theme is again subjected to various contrapuntal manipulations, where different countersubjects are fitted to the opening bars of the theme. The orchestra at bb. 687–91, in four real parts, is especially effective. At b. 694, B♭ minor is replaced by the parallel major. The tonic is reached at b. 695, but a neighbouring chord of G (VI) – a reference to the G tonality of the opening of the *Dies iræ* movement? – interrupts the tonic major. The movement concludes with low-lying chords played tutti, with the third of the chord on top. Verdi employs here and in the *Lux æterna* two effects that he might have learned from Berlioz's treatise on orchestration: the pedal-tone B♭₁ in Trombone 3, and the dyads played by two timpani.

5

Offertorio

Offertorio: A quattro voci (Soprano, Mezzo-Soprano, Tenore e Basso). Orchestra: tutti, minus bass drum. A♭ major; 222 bars (*c.* 7'45")

Antiphon: Domine Jesu Christe, Rex gloriæ, libera animas omnium fidelium defunctorum de pœnis inferni, et de profundo lacu: libera eas de ore leonis, ne absorbeat eas tartarus, ne cadant in obscurum: sed signifer sanctus Michael repræsentet eas in lucem sanctam.

Quam olim Abrahæ promisisti et semini ejus.

Verse: Hostias et preces tibi, Domine, laudis offerimus: tu suscipe pro animabus illis, quarum hodie memoriam facimus: fac eas, Domine, de morte transire ad vitam.

Quam olim Abrahæ promisisti et semini ejus.

[Libera animas omnium fidelium defunctorum de pœnis inferni. Fac eas de morte transire ad vitam.]

Antiphon: O Lord, Jesus Christ, King of glory, deliver the souls of all the departed faithful from the torments of hell and from the bottomless pit; deliver them from the mouth of the lion; lest Tartarus swallow them; lest they fall into the darkness. But let Saint Michael the standard-bearer bring them forth into the holy light.

Which thou didst once promise unto Abraham and his seed.

Verse: To thee, O Lord, we render our offerings and prayers with praise. Do thou receive them for those souls which we commemorate today. Make them, O Lord, pass from death unto life.

Which Thou didst once promise unto Abraham and his seed.

[Deliver the souls of all the departed faithful from the torments of hell. Make them pass from death unto life.]

Fig. 5.1 *Offertorio* text

While the Offertories in most Requiems, including those of Mozart and Cherubini, follow the liturgical text by ending with the return of the 'Quam olim Abrahæ' section, Verdi concludes with a much-abbreviated reprise of the opening section, set to text conflated from antiphon and verse. While there is no *a priori* reason to prefer structures with a reprise of the opening (Verdi's ABCBA' arch form) to those without it (the ABCB or ABCB' designs found in Mozart and Cherubini), in Verdi's *Offertorio* the musical reprise has an

45

important function: by revisiting the A material Verdi resolves tensions left unresolved in that first section.

A 'Domine Jesu Christe' – bb. 1–88. A♭ major; Andante mosso, $\frac{6}{8}$ ($\downarrow$. = 66); 88 bars (2'45")

This section consists of three phases: the invocation to the Lord ('Domine Jesu Christe', mezzo-soprano and tenor), a plea for deliverance from the vividly described terrors of Hell ('Libera animas', marked by the entrance of the bass), and finally the positive image of Salvation (the soprano's entrance with 'sed signifer sanctus Michael'). Despite the violent contrast of imagery, virtually all the musical material in this section is derived from the 'dolce' and 'cantabile' phrase played by the cellos (bb. 13ff.). In the second phase, Mozart and Cherubini depict the terrors incisively, but Verdi's setting may seem unusually restrained. Budden speaks of a 'mood of almost unclouded serenity', and Hussey finds that there is 'none of that sense of physical terror [found at the opening of *Libera me*] for all that the poetic idea is at one point the same'.[1] (Perhaps the difference is that here the text lacks the first-person pronoun; the speaker seems not to be in imminent danger and does not emerge as a character.)

Despite the lack of thematic contrast, however, one should not underestimate the tension that Verdi generates in this phase, nor the amount of contrast with the final phase (even though it is less than that in the settings of Mozart and Cherubini). For Verdi finds other means to suggest the terrors of Hell: at the first mention of the 'pœnis inferni', the music darkens, turning to the minor mode. The line 'libera eas de ore leonis' is built upon excited overlapping entrances of the opening bar of the theme. The passage then collapses into a half cadence in F minor, but that key will not be achieved until the 'Quam olim Abrahæ' section. The soprano, evoking St. Michael and initiating the final phase, enters on a long-held e♮[2] (first heard as the leading tone of F minor), over which two solo violins hauntingly play the principal theme, in the process reinterpreting the harmonic implications of the note and sliding to remote tonal regions. A further semitonal slide rehearses a singular harmonic progression heard moments before the end of *Rigoletto*.[2] This third phase eventually returns to the tonic, but there is no strong sense of closure. There are few strong cadences in the A section, and none of them is in the tonic. Indeed, there is no root-position tonic triad until six bars before the end (b. 82), and it is approached by a weak V$^4_3$–I cadence built on a stepwise descending bass line; the two plagal cadences that follow offer little additional support.

B 'Quam olim Abrahæ' – bb. 89–118. F minor → A♭ major; Allegro mosso, 𝄵 (♩ = 152); 29 bars (*c.* 45″)

The line 'Quam olim Abrahæ promisisti et semini ejus' is traditionally set as a fugue, as in works of Michael Haydn, Mozart, Cherubini, and Dvořák (though not Berlioz or Fauré). Verdi settled for an emblem of *stile antico*: a point of imitation on a two-bar motive, upon which all of the voices enter in turn.[3] The tempo is brisk, the only fast piece for soloists. After all the voices have entered (b. 97), all pretence of counterpoint is abandoned. A broad chromatic theme, sweeping through a twelfth and characterized by rapid harmonic rhythm, is presented three times in different colourful harmonizations, and with increasing intensity: in performing forces employed, dynamic level, and level of rhythmic activity in the accompaniment (from steady quarters, to eighth-note rhythm, and finally to triplet eighth-notes). The third statement ends with a deceptive cadence, and a short transition wrenches from A♭ major to C major and drops from *fortissimo* to *ppp*.

C 'Hostias' – bb. 118–62. C major; Adagio, 𝄵 (♩ = 66); 45 bars (*c.* 2′45″)

Hussey claimed that the 'Hostias' would surely convince anyone who might still doubt 'Verdi's ability to express genuine religious feeling', and other writers have also approvingly written along the lines that the melody 'has the economy and the texture of plainsong'.[4] Writers concerned about the work's supposed theatricality tend to rhapsodize over every diatonic melody with small range and conjunct motion. Filippi first described the tenor's melody as having a religious character, but unfolding dramatically, in a later review describing it as being in the 'stile *Aidiano*'.[5] Plainsong and *Aida* may seem a curious mix, but the two conceptions are not necessarily contradictory: according to another Italian critic the main theme evoked a 'mystic sentiment' and 'an antique world as in the invocation to immenso Ftà in *Aida*'.[6] The theme is clearly related to the opening vocal phrase in Act III of *Aida* ('O tu che sei d'Osiride' – another religious ceremony), as it is also to the 'Ingemisco' and the *Agnus Dei* (which of course also shares its key of C major, the most serene key in the *Requiem*). By citing their principal motive (stepwise motion through a third and back) in the mock litany in *Falstaff* (Act III scene ii), Verdi himself associated these themes with a 'religious style'.

The melody is calm, but not motionless or without purposeful direction. It starts tentatively with a two-bar motive, tries again with more success, expanding to a four-bar phrase, and then, on the third attempt – 'animando' – flowers into a complete musical idea, finally expanding the narrow range, reaching a melodic climax on g^1 and descending gracefully to c^1. The harmonization stresses the modal degrees (ii, iii, and vi), with iii^6 even used as a substitute for V (b. 124). Despite the emphasis on e^1 and c^1 (the root and third of the tonic triad), there are only two root-position triads, and only at the end is there a strong authentic cadence.

This theme dominates the rondo-like structure of the 'Hostias': the two minor-mode episodes function as dark clouds to be swept away by – and to justify – additional statements of the main theme. After the bass repeats the theme in F major (IV) – its only complete restatement – there is a short episode in G minor (v) consisting of two three-bar phrases, and a return of the theme, reduced to its first and last phrases. Another minor-mode episode (bb. 151–9), this one based upon the principal motive, is again followed by a return to the main theme, now represented by its first bar alone, played three times by the solo flute. As elsewhere in the 'Hostias' (and in the entire *Offertorio*) the orchestration is remarkable: here there are violin harmonics, tremolo in the second violins and violas, with the lower strings marking the downbeat with a pizzicato. Solo oboe and horn inflect $\hat{5}$ from a grace-note a semitone below. In the middle of this five-octave span, the singers chant their prayer on repeated notes.

B 'Quam olim Abrahæ' – bb. 163–97. Come prima (*c*. 1')

The reprise is virtually exact, the orchestral parts simply being cued to the initial statement.[7] An expanded transition leads to the abbreviated reprise of the opening.

A' 'Libera animas' – bb. 198–222. Come prima (*c*. 45")

The first section was tonally unstable; now the task is to ground it by presenting its thematic material solidly in the tonic. As in the 'Rex tremendæ majestatis', the thematic reprise functions as a resolution.[8] The four soloists sing three statements of the main theme, in unison and octaves over a tonic pedal.[9] The strings play the progression Ab–f–c, summarizing the principal tonal centres in the movement (bb. 206–7). The soprano now rises from c^1 to ab^2 in a free inversion of the second bar of the principal theme – the journey 'de morte . . . ad vitam'? In the opening section the theme was harmonized quite simply – usually with tonic and dominant chords (although, as noted above, never with a root-position tonic chord). At the conclusion of the movement, with the stability of the theme finally guaranteed, Verdi can afford to present it in melting reharmonizations.

6

Sanctus

Sanctus: Fuga a due Cori. Orchestra: tutti, minus bass drum. F major; Allegro,
C ($\rfloor$ =138), followed by Allegro, **¢** ($\rfloor$ = 112); 139 bars (*c*. 2'30"–2'45")

Sanctus, sanctus, sanctus,	Holy, Holy, Holy,
Dominus Deus Sabaoth!	Lord God of Hosts!
Pleni sunt cœli et terra gloria tua,	Heaven and earth are full of Thy glory,
Hosanna in excelsis.	Hosanna in the highest.
Benedictus qui venit	Blessed is he that cometh
in nomine Domini,	in the name of the Lord
Hosanna in excelsis.	Hosanna in the highest.

Verdi's *Sanctus*, an exuberant fugue for double chorus, contrasts sharply with
the movements of his predecessors. First, as opposed to the slow tempos and
(in several instances) 'maestoso' character of the *Sanctus* movements of the
Requiems Verdi knew – and that of the prospectus for the *Messa per Rossini*[1]
– Verdi's movement proceeds at breakneck speed. His exclamation mark at
the end of the first line is indicative of his conception.

The fugal texture is uncommon as well, although the Requiems of Mozart
and Berlioz follow tradition in having a fugal 'Hosanna' contrasting with the
homophonic texture of the rest of the movement. And, while in those works
there are distinct sections (or even separate movements) for the 'Hosanna' and
'Benedictus', Verdi treats the text as projecting a single joyous affect.[2]

Verdi's approach to fugue requires some clarification. When we listen to
Bach's fugues, we have learned to discern, at any given moment, whether or
not the 'subject' is present. There is a tendency to privilege the subject, as
is clear from the practice of designating as 'episodes' those passages where it
is absent, and generations of pianists have been taught to thump out the
subject on its every appearance. By 'subject' I, of course, mean the subject in
its entirety, for Bach's episodes are often derived from it. There is therefore
an opposition and tension between presentations of the complete subject and
the episodes.

This would not be an appropriate way to listen to the two fugues in
Verdi's *Requiem*, however.[3] After a textbook exposition – with tonal answers,

49

consistent use of countersubjects and without episodes (or 'codettas') separating appearances of the subject – Verdi tosses the textbook aside. The subject is soon pared down to shorter versions – usually beginning with its opening motive – and these may, *faute de mieux*, 'stand for' the subject. These abbreviated statements of the subject then dominate the rest of the fugue: the countersubjects so prominent in the exposition are undercut or even discarded early on, and passages lacking even these abbreviated statements of the subject are rare or non-existent. It is therefore useful to include both complete and incomplete statements as presentations of the subject, reserving 'episode' for passages lacking even an abbreviated statement of the subject.[4] 'Fugal devices' such as inversion, augmentation, and stretto play a large role after the exposition. Tonally, these fugues are tripartite: the tonally stable first section, consisting primarily of the exposition, is followed by a modulatory middle section in which the tonic is avoided, and a final section, in which the tonic reigns unchallenged.

The *Sanctus* begins with a short (eight-bar) introduction with trumpet calls. After a quick exchange between Chorus 1 and Chorus 2, the introduction ends with a *fortissimo* shout of 'Sanctus' on a dominant-seventh chord.

In the first section of the fugue (bb. 9–33) each chorus presents, simultaneously with the other, an independent fugal exposition, each with its own subject and set of countersubjects, the voices in each chorus entering from top to bottom: sopranos, altos, tenors, then basses.[5] While most strands of the orchestra restrict themselves to doubling the vocal lines, a playful variant of Subject 2, marked '*leggere e staccate*', moves through the strings and up to the woodwinds during the course of the exposition (see Violin 1 at bb. 10–14 for its first appearance). This contrast between scampering continuous motion in the orchestra and the vigorous – or later, expressive – vocal lines is an important characteristic of this movement.

After the fugal exposition and a counter-exposition of two additional entrances, much of the rigorous contrapuntal framework is cast aside. Furthermore, unlike the exposition, the two choruses now share the same musical material, reducing the contrast between them. The chorus definitively abandons Subject 2, although the orchestra will later remind us of its scampering *moto perpetuo* variant; the countersubjects are never heard again. Even more surprising, a complete statement of Subject 1 never reappears, although few passages lack reference to some element of the subject. At b. 33 there explodes a *fortissimo* mock-stretto passage based on the initial arpeggio of Subject 1; through a sleight-of-hand modulation this leads to a strong cadence in vi.

The middle section (bb. 41–78, almost a third of the fugue's length) is developmental, with much modulation and frequent use of stretto (as before, based on a truncated version of Subject 1 but now accompanied by the scampering variant of Subject 2 in the strings). Although this section is taken up entirely with a new text not used elsewhere in the movement – 'Benedictus qui venit in nomine Domini' – it is not comparable to a separate 'Benedictus' section or movement. Except for the modulatory activity, the textures and material are not radically different from the previous passage, and if the music drops to a *piano* dynamic at the introduction of the text it soon enough flares up into violent *fortissimo* stretto passages.

This leads back to the tonic, which will prevail in this final section of the fugue (bb. 79–139, nearly half of its length), and to the reintroduction of the text 'Pleni sunt coeli et terra gloria tua', sung by Chorus 1, which is urged on by Chorus 2 with its cries of 'Hosanna'. It would be hard to imagine a sharper contrast from the preceding section. This final section begins with an expressive augmentation – at first 'dolcissimo' and 'espressivo' – of the second to fourth bars of Subject 1, sung by Chorus 1 (bb. 79–110). In the middle section the subject had been represented only by the vigorous ascending arpeggio (the first bar), but now for this lyrical moment Verdi singles out for treatment the more expressive balancing stepwise descent. The texture is simplified to homophony.

Many of the augmentation sections in Bach's fugues feature stretto with the subject presented simultaneously at its normal pace – a contrapuntal logjam. Verdi's augmentation passages are expressive thematic transformations rather than manifestations of climactic contrapuntal artifice. At this point in the *Sanctus* the effect is that of a sudden halving of the tempo, since no strand of the texture preserves the original pace (at least before b. 109). The phrasing is not only regular, but the thirty-two-bar period is divided into the clearest example of the 'lyric prototype' in the entire *Requiem*;[6] the lyric prototype is of course designed for setting Italian poetry, generally two four-line stanzas. Its appearance in a fugue, a setting of a sacred text in Latin prose, is highly marked, and it is reasonable to suppose that both Verdi and his audience would have recognized it as an emblem of tradition and therefore as an additional element conferring stability.

Towards the end of the *Sanctus* fugue then – and, as will be seen, that of the *Libera me* fugue – the subject is treated in various ways that lead to stability and closure. Although it would be puzzling to speak of a 'reprise' in movements where the principal theme is hardly ever absent, Verdi's strategy is clearly analogous to the procedure I have termed 'reprise as resolution' in the 'Rex tremendæ', *Offertorio*, and *Lux æterna* (see below).

At the end of this period a wisp of the theme's first four bars in the winds recall the initial arpeggio motive of Subject 1, the scampering variant of Subject 2, and the original tempo (bb. 109–14). The rest of the movement is a boisterous peroration, with the voices generally proceeding in steady half-notes starting with a descending scale (which Verdi has by now trained us to accept as motivic) and proceeding to shapes that we are willing to accept as derived, in turn, from the motivic F-major scale. Simply by extending the opening four-note chromatic ascent of the scampering motive, Verdi dissolves this motive into frantic chromatic eighth-note scales in the whole orchestra. Near the end of the movement the sopranos of Chorus 1 carry the line to high $b\flat^2$ and close on the tonic, but the phrase nonetheless seems unresolved, as the expected a^2 has been postponed, the dissonant $b\flat^2$ left hanging (bb. 130–1). After an equally frantic syncopated ascent in the orchestra, the sopranos fill in the missing a^2 – emphasized with a fermata erroneously omitted in many editions – and the movement comes to a close.

7

Agnus Dei

Agnus Dei: A due voci (Soprano e Mezzo–Soprano) e Coro. Orchestra: woodwinds (with a third flute rather than piccolo), horns, and strings. C major; Andante, **C** (♩ = 84); 74 bars (*c.* 3'30")

Agnus Dei, qui tollis peccata mundi, dona eis requiem;	Lamb of God, that takest away the sins of the world, grant them rest.
Agnus Dei, qui tollis peccata mundi, dona eis requiem;	Lamb of God, that takest away the sins of the world, grant them rest.
Agnus Dei, qui tollis peccata mundi, dona eis requiem sempiternam.	Lamb of God, that takest away the sins of the world, grant them eternal rest.

Verdi set the *Agnus Dei* and the *Lux æterna* (the Communion) as two separate movements, following Mozart and the *Messa per Rossini* prospectus rather than Cherubini and Berlioz, who incorporated the two texts into a single movement. Mozart and Cherubini had contrasted an anguished evocation with a calmer plea for mercy, 'dona eis requiem', a strategy which recalls their, and Verdi's, settings of the 'Rex tremendæ majestatis'. However, as in the *Sanctus*, Verdi chose to express a single affect for the entire text: here he set each of the three petitions as a single serene period without internal contrasts. The dynamic range of this lightly scored movement ranges from *ppp* to *p*, and its structure is a theme and variations, one of the most placid of all musical forms, well suited to impart a sense of calm and timelessness. Moreover, it is a particularly static type (cantus firmus variations): aside from slight changes for the minor-mode variation, the theme, sung by soloists and chorus, remains unchanged until the coda; it is the orchestral accompaniment surrounding the theme that changes.[1] An antiphonal procedure is superimposed upon the variation structure: the chorus responds to each of the soloists' petitions, first with a complete statement of the theme (a complete variation), then, after the second and third petitions, with a variation of only the final phrase of the theme.

The two soloists sing nothing but the theme (or fragments of it), and invariably sing it in octaves, except at the very end, when they finally join at the unison. The two soloists must blend well, assuming a single musical persona, as did Stolz and Waldmann, according to one commentator: 'so perfectly did they sing together that it was like one voice. Their styles are as near alike as it is possible for a contralto and soprano to be.'[2]

Much of the effect of the movement depends on the theme. It is subtly crafted, allowing for repeated hearings.

Ex. 7.1   *Agnus Dei*, bb. 1–13

The first phrase (a, four bars) is marked by stepwise motion circling back upon itself, a feature shared by the 'Ingemisco' and especially by the 'Hostias'. While the first phrase was constrained within the interval of a perfect fourth, the second phrase (b, three bars) immediately pushes the line to G and ends by taking it to its low point an octave lower. The eighth-notes at the end of its first bar spill over into the first half of the second, so that its course is traversed in only three bars. It would have been child's play to patch together a four-bar consequent phrase, or, failing that, to balance the seven-bar period with a conclusion of equal length, but Verdi's final phrase (a', six bars, with a caesura in the middle of the fourth bar), like the second (b), ends one bar earlier than expected. After a feint to ii (the c♯ is the only non-diatonic note in the melody) and the caesura, the line reaches its peak on A and floats down in eighth-note motion checked only at the cadence, a diminution of the cadence figure at the end of the second phrase. The flexibility of the phrase structure contributes to the affinity with plainchant that many writers have sensed.[3]

Verdi seems to have fashioned the theme almost as though it were a purely instrumental melody. Not only is there extensive word repetition, but he altered the text underlay in the course of the movement: in the third and tenth bars of the theme he had originally placed the second syllable of 'Agnus' or 'dona' on the third beat. And in both surviving albumleaves with the first four bars of the *Agnus Dei*, he misremembered the declamation, placing 'qui tollis' in the third and fourth bars.

The events of the movement might be summarized as follows: **Soloists' first petition (Theme)**: The soprano and mezzo-soprano present the theme in octaves, unaccompanied. **First choral response (Variation 1)**: A restatement of the theme, still unharmonized, presented in the middle and low register of the chorus, doubled by the clarinets, bassoons, and strings. **Soloists' second petition (Variation 2)**: In this *minore* variation the orchestra (syncopated solo flute and clarinet, with violas and cellos harmonizing the theme) first emerges as an independent voice, rather than merely doubling the vocal parts. **Second choral response (Variation 2a – a' phrase only)**: *Maggiore*, with chorus (sopranos and altos with the theme in octaves, the tenors and basses providing harmonic filler) and orchestra (minus flutes, kept in reserve for the next section). The opening chord, the first tonic major triad in the movement, is a most expressive moment. The harmonization of the theme that follows features rich secondary dominants in the first half of the phrase, and, in the last two bars, a rather modal-sounding progression (V^7–vi–iii–V^7–I). **Soloists' third petition (Variation 3)**: The soloists' presentation of the theme is now garlanded by the three flutes in continuous eighth-note motion, a passage praised by some of the earliest critics and 'quoted in every book on instrumentation'.[4] At this point Verdi moves to the text of the final prayer, adding 'sempiternam' at the close.

Third choral response (Variation 3a – a' phrase only): This is similar to the second choral response, with a countermelody in the violins which continues the eighth-note motion of the preceding variation. At the end, the two soloists at last add their voices to the chorus. **Coda**: The coda is built upon two transformations of the final subphrase (bb. 64–7, 67–72), with the descending arpeggio replacing the descending eighth-notes of the theme. After the tenors' arpeggio ends with a questioning leap to scale degree $\hat{6}$ (a♮), the two soloists, still in octaves, reply with the final cadence of the theme. On its repetition, the basses' arpeggio concludes with the more intense ♭$\hat{6}$ (A♭),[5] momentarily suggesting a mysterious augmented triad. But the two soloists ignore the threat: finally joining in unison, they sing the cadence in augmentation.

8

Lux æterna

Lux æterna: A tre voci (Mezzo-Soprano, Tenore e Basso). Orchestra: tutti, minus trumpets. B♭ major; Molto moderato, **C** (♩ = 88); 105 bars (*c.* 4'45")

Antiphon:	1. Lux æterna luceat	*Antiphon*:	Let eternal light shine
	eis, Domine,		upon them, O Lord,
	2. cum Sanctis tuis		with Thy saints
	in æternum,		in eternity,
	3. quia pius es.		for Thou art merciful.
Verse:	1. Requiem æternam	*Verse*:	Grant them eternal rest,
	dona eis, Domine		O Lord,
	2. et lux perpetua		and let perpetual light
	luceat eis.		shine upon them.
	3. Cum Sanctis tuis		With Thy saints
	in æternum,		in eternity,
	4. quia pius es.		for Thou art merciful.
	[Lux perpetua luceat eis,		[Let perpetual light shine upon them,
	Domine. Requiem æternam.]		O Lord. Eternal rest.]

The verse begins with an exact repetition of the Introit antiphon ('Requiem æternam . . .') and a number of Requiems incorporate a musical reprise of the first movement here, such as those of Michael Haydn, Mozart/Süssmayr, and Berlioz, all of which conclude with the *Lux æterna*. Since Verdi's *Requiem* ends instead with the *Libera me*, which also repeats this text, he chose to postpone the musical reprise.

Although some Requiems (including those of Cherubini, Dvořák, and Fauré) omit from the verse the repetition of 'Cum sanctis tuis in æternum, quia pius est' present in the liturgical text, the phrase is included in Mozart's *Requiem* (as the final fugue), in the text given in the *Messa per Rossini* prospectus, and in Verdi's movement. The bracketed extra-liturgical text conflates the antiphon ('Lux æterna luceat eis, Domine') and verse ('Requiem æternam . . . Lux *perpetua* luceat eis' of the antiphon). The movement might be best outlined as follows: A B C B' D D' D" A'.

A 1–15 (Antiphon: mezzo-soprano, strings). The mezzo-soprano declaims the antiphon text, accompanied by tremolos in the twenty-four violins, subdivided to provide six-note chords, suggesting to some writers 'a shimmer of light'. The first ten measures, controlled neither by functional root progressions nor by firmly sculpted linear motion, constitute the most extreme example of harmonic mystification in the entire *Requiem*. The tremolos in divided violins, the arcane harmonic progression, and the textual image of sacred light recall Jean's invocation 'Que la sainte lumière descende sur ton front . . .' from the exorcism in Meyerbeer's *Le Prophète*, a scene Verdi admired.[1] After the initial I_4^6 – a striking way to open a movement – the harmonic progression veers away, reaching in bb. 5–6 a D-major triad (later rationalized as V/vi). The only salient melodic event in bb. 1–6 is a rising then falling third (d^2–$f\sharp^2$–d^2) high in the mezzo-soprano's range. She continues to govern bb. 7–10, repeating in sequence the falling third motive – c^2–a^1; $g\sharp^1$–e^1 – harmonized in a way that defies functional analysis. Will I be accused of politically incorrect ethnic stereotyping if I suggest that it seems typically Italian – or at least un-German – that in the absence of a functional harmonic progression, it is the vocal line (here the upper voice) – rather than the bass line – that provides an Ariadne's thread through the passage? Although the strings double the mezzo-soprano, the melodic line with its sequence – the only element that provides coherence – is perceived to be hers. At bb. 10–11, the harmonic progression gets back on track, moving first through a circle of fifths momentarily inflecting vi (the G-minor triad in b.12) then moving purposefully to the strong cadence in B♭ at b. 16.[2] In the process, the mezzo-soprano presents a diatonic variant of the motive she sang earlier – now d^2– $f\natural^2$–d^2 – then ending on $b\flat^1$. Thus she starts from chaos, but regains control and achieves partial stability, even though this is then undermined by the bass's turn to minor on the text 'Requiem æternam'. This raises other sources of tension that will demand resolution later.

B 15–26 (Verse, line 1: soloists, with bass dominating; winds and timpani). As in the first movement, Verdi contrasts the two images: 'Lux', consolatory and in the major mode, with 'Requiem', mournful and in the minor mode, here a funeral march, with dotted rhythms and an effectively sombre scoring, a hollow open fifth roll on two timpani punctuated by ominous low-lying chords in bassoons and low brass. The bass cadences deceptively on VI (G♭), enharmonically equivalent to the F♯ that the mezzo-soprano inflected in the A section as well as the (local) tonic of the C section.

C 27–42 (Verse, lines 2–4: the three soloists, unaccompanied). 'Lux' again brings consolation, and the key brightens from i to VI (from b♭ to G♭). Although the major mode partially counters the lugubrious tone of the B♭ minor of the preceding section, a section in the tonic will be needed to provide resolution.

B' 43–53 (Repeat of Verse, line 1: soloists, with the bass dominating). This reprise is intensified: B consisted of two six-bar units (each consisting of 3 x 2 bars), while B' compresses this into two four-bar units, the last bar elided with a final asymmetrical three-bar group. The orchestration is also more intense, with the addition of tremolo strings (middle and low register), and *pianissimo* bass drum with double-basses (pizzicato, *forte*) marking the downbeat, along with bassoons and low brass.

D 54–67 (Repeat of Verse, lines 2–4: mezzo-soprano). A consolatory new theme sung *dolcissimo* by the mezzo-soprano ends another cycle of *chiaroscuro* with the gloomy 'Requiem' assuaged by 'Lux'. This section marks the return of B♭ major, although a strong cadence is not achieved until the end of the section. Her line, doubled by the flutes, is the lowest part; above there are string tremolos and an oscillating figure played two octaves higher by first violins and piccolo. One reviewer wrote that while the B section 'froze one's blood with dark thoughts . . . [at the D section] it seemed that the heaven opened up, such is the sweetness of the effect of a light, spiritual, indefinite orchestration'.[3] And yet the consolation offered by the return to the tonic and the lyrical melody is undercut by the deceptive cadence and startling *fortissimo* chord that soon follow.

D' 67–83 (Repeat of Verse, lines 3–4: soloists). The bass now takes up the mezzo-soprano's melody (though with different text), with the mezzo-soprano and tenor taking a supporting role at first. Solo flute and clarinet play arpeggios, a figuration sufficiently distinctive that its reappearance later can serve to recall the passage. This section ends with a cadential phrase (on 'quia pius es') that will recur in the Act II Quartet of *Otello*.

D" 84–94 (Repeat of Verse, lines 3–4: the soloists, unaccompanied). This begins with an imitative treatment of the theme introduced in D, but immediately gives way to a free continuation, one rather more contrapuntal (though non-imitative) than was section C. Like the final section, D" refers back to different sections: here by combining the thematic material of D with the scoring of C.

A' (with references to B and D)   94–105 (the bracketed extra-liturgical text: mezzo-soprano, with tenor and bass). The reprise of the A section resolves elements from the movement as a whole, specifically the tonally unstable section A and the minor-mode section B. The clearest reference is to the opening of section A: accompanied by tremolos in the divided upper strings, the mezzo-soprano intones 'Lux perpetua luceat eis, Domine'; ignoring her initial chromatic d^2–f♯^{2}–d^2, she opts for the diatonic version d^2–f♮^{2}–d^2, then continuing on to b♭^{1}. The D-major triad (III/B♭) recalls the *recherché* harmonies of the opening, but now tamed and rationalized. The D–major chord does not lead further astray, nor does it even threaten to tonicize vi: it and the D–minor triad in b. 99 are merely neighbouring chords governed by the strongly established tonic B♭. The recall of elements associated with the unstable section A helps to resolve the tensions of that section.

Similarly, since the low brass and timpani have appeared only in the B and B' sections, their reappearance here, coupled with the tenor and bass intoning 'Requiem æternam', suffices to establish the reference to those two sections, even though their characteristic melody and minor mode are absent. Here too, the recall and neutralization of menacing elements serves to exorcize them.[4]

9

The Libera me *and its genesis*

Libera me: Solo per Soprano, Cori, e Fuga finale. C minor; 1869: 391 bars (11'15"–11'45"); 1874: 421 bars (11'45"–12'30")

Although the discussion here focuses on the definitive 1874 *Libera me*, I consider a few of the most significant revisions of the 1869 movement as well.[1] Both versions may be divided into four principal sections:

I   Declamatory solo for soprano ('Libera me, Domine')

II   Chorus ('Dies iræ, dies illa') – in 1874 a reprise of the 'Dies iræ music'

III   Soprano solo and chorus, unaccompanied ('Requiem æternam') – in 1874 a reprise of the antiphon of the 'Requiem æternam'

IVa   Transition to fugue

IVb   Fugue (chorus with solos for the soprano)

Section I: 'Libera me' (1869: 1–41; 1874: 1–44). Declamatory solo for soprano (chorus appears in only four bars). Orchestra: woodwind, horns, trombones (1874 only), percussion, and strings. C minor; Moderato, **C** ($\downarrow$ = 72); 1869: 41 bars (*c.* 2'30"); 1874: 44 bars (2'30"–2'45")

Respond: Libera me, Domine, de morte æterna, in die illa tremenda: quando cœli movendi sunt et terra. Dum veneris judicare sæculum per ignem.	*Respond*: Save me, Lord, from eternal death on that momentous day when heaven and earth are moved, when Thou shalt come to judge the world through fire.
Verse: Tremens factus sum ego et timeo, dum discussio venerit atque ventura ira, quando cœli movendi sunt et terra.	*Verse*: Trembling I am made, and I fear when the separation shall come and the coming anger, when heaven and earth are moved.

The opening depicts a supplicant chanting in plainsong, but the evocation of church music is immediately abandoned: the neutral monotone chant gives way in b. 4 to a forceful declamation, intensified by the crescendo, as though the soprano has suddenly unburdened herself of emotion hitherto suppressed.

The harmonic progression, which may recall the opening of *Rigoletto* Act I scene ii, establishes C minor as the tonic, but withholds the tonic triad, not to appear until b. 20. The chorus, representing a group of supplicants, responds in *falsobordone* on E♭, then sinking in parallel triads to the Neapolitan D♭. Bars 11–14 abruptly pull back to the dominant, a tritone away, the soprano declaiming the remainder of the first part of the Respond over the presentation of an important motive of the 'Dies iræ music' – the music of these four bars will return near the close of Section II (see Ex. 11.3c). The motive repeats itself, as though at first unable to continue, then frees itself on the third try.

The passage for four bassoons finally provides the long-awaited cadence in C minor (bb. 15–20). Verdi sets up the cadence in b. 16, but in the next bar avoids it by a sudden thinning of the texture. A remarkable one-bar harmonic parenthesis moves far afield before the dominant is vigorously reasserted with a *forte* unison.[2]

Most of the remainder of the section is set as a 'parlante melodico' – in which the orchestra presents the principal melodic material, the singer(s) declaiming against it, but on occasion doubling the instrumental melody.[3] Although *parlanti* are common in Verdi's operas, this is one of the few examples in the *Requiem*. Here, as at the opening of the movement, the singer progresses from monotone declamation to an explosion of grief and fear. As she stammers 'Tremens factus sum ego', the first violins and flutes obsessively circle around g^1 for two bars,[4] then the singer leaps to the tonic and, in a passage that recalls the 'Quam olim Abrahæ' of the *Offertorio*, descends chromatically in rapid harmonic rhythm. The performative nature of her stammering so strongly establishes the soprano as a character speaking in her own, female voice, that we overlook the masculine ending, 'fact*us*', with which she refers to herself, just as we quickly forgot that the text that the mezzo-soprano stammered so effectively in the 'Liber scriptus' was in the third person. Verdi's revision of the remainder of the first section repays scrutiny. Ex. 9.1 presents the vocal lines and a partial harmonic analysis for the remainder of this first section.

For now, however, the discussion will be confined to 1869: 19–35/1874: 20–36, and primarily to the orchestral framework. Most of the changes in this section can be regarded as parts of a more comprehensive plan designed to strengthen the sense of arrival at the cadences at 1874: 33 and 40. These cadences, two of only three authentic cadences in the section, occur at important points in its structure – the return of the 'Tremens factus' phrase and the close of the section.

The crucial difference between the two versions occurs at 1869: 30–1/1874:

Ex. 9.1   Soprano part of *Libera me*, 1869: bb. 19–41 / 1874: bb. 20–44
(↓ = authentic cadence)

32–3, where a cadence introduces a return of the first phrase of the example. In the 1869 version, the dominant preparation seems insufficient, but in the 1874 version Verdi extends the dominant to 1874: 32, thus postponing the cadence and the reprise by one bar. Not only does this extra bar of dominant provide a crucial increment of dominant harmony, but it dissolves the harmonic pattern established in the previous bars – a rocking back and forth between V^7/V (the dominant of the dominant) and V^7 – signalling that V^7 is finally ready to resolve to the tonic.[5] In the 1874 version the 'reversal', as Leonard Meyer has called the breaking of an insistent harmonic or thematic pattern,[6] occurs *before* the cadence, giving the listener time to prepare for the inevitable arrival. This change in 1869: 31 / 1874: 32 serves to break up another pattern as well, one working on a higher level: the phrase structure. Verdi has set up a scheme of what may be described as overlapping five-bar phrases: the deceptive cadences on the downbeat of 1869: 23, 27 / 1874: 24, 28 both complete one phrase and begin the next. In the 1869 version, this pattern continues almost to the end of the example (i.e., until 1869: 35), but in the revised version the third phrase has been extended to six bars (1874: 28–33), overlapping the following four-bar phrase (1874: 33–6), a compressed statement of the opening five-bar phrase. The repositioning of the five-beat 'Tremens factus sum ego' declamation to begin on the downbeat of b. 33, rather than two beats later, seems to be a result of this strategy.

Verdi's revision of the close of the first section exemplifies a recurring strategy in the 1874 version (1869: 35–41 / 1874: 35–44 – see Ex. 9.1). In 1869 Verdi extended the return of the 'Tremens factus' phrase by an additional two bars, but the ending nonetheless sounds abrupt. In the 1874 version he spun out yet another two bars, in which the soprano has a strong closing gesture (1874: 38–9) that clearly anticipates the coming fugue subject. Again and again, the role of the soprano soloist is greatly enhanced in the revised version – Verdi found a number of opportunities to give her material previously allotted to the chorus, or, as in this case, to add new material to her part. This occurs most frequently at important moments in the structure, such as at the end of a section, or the transition from one section to another. Verdi was now writing for a soprano with power throughout her range and puts that power to good use.[7] Furthermore, the prospectus for the 1869 *Messa per Rossini* specifies that the *Libera me* was to be scored for 'Coro con *a soli* per soprano' (chorus with solos for soprano), a formulation which de-emphasizes the role of the soloist. But in the 1874 version, Verdi was free from the dictates of the committee for the *Messa per Rossini* and could go his own way: his preferred designation for the 1874 movement was 'Solo per soprano e cori e fuga finale'.

Another symptom of the change in approach is that, in the original version, the soprano was required to sing with the sopranos of the chorus much more often than in the definitive version.

Section II: 'Dies iræ' (1869: 42–103; 1874: 45–131). Chorus (in 1869 the soprano soloist doubles the choral sopranos for the first forty bars; in both versions there is a solo for seven bars on the text 'Dum veneris judicare sæculum per ignem', a reprise of the same text and music in Section I. In the 1874 version the first sixty-one bars of this section are a reprise of the opening of the 'Dies iræ'.) Orchestra: tutti (both versions). 1869: C minor; Allegro agitato, Lo stesso movimento col tempo raddoppiato, ¢ (♩=144); 62 bars (1'45"); 1874: G minor; Allegro agitato, ¢ (♩= 80); 87 bars (*c*. 2'15").

Verse: Dies iræ, dies illa,[8]	*Verse*: Day of wrath, that day
calamitatis et miseriæ,	of calamity and wretchedness,
dies magna et amara valde.	day both great and too bitter,
Dum veneris judicare	when Thou shalt come to judge the
sæculum per ignem.	world through fire.

Like the second reprise (following the 'Confutatis maledictis'), the final reprise of the 'Dies iræ' is a cataclysmic disruption, arriving unexpectedly, without dominant preparation.[9] The most fundamental revision in the entire movement is Verdi's replacement of the first ten bars of the 'Dies iræ' section of the 1869 *Libera me* (Ex. 9.2) with thirty newly composed bars (1874: 45–74), the only thematic material in the 1874 *Libera me* not already present in the 1869 movement. The principal reason for the revision was probably the tonal instability of the 1869 form of this passage. The tonally ambiguous, modulating theme of the 1869 version might have been suitable in the *middle* of the *Libera me* movement, but it would not do as the *opening* of the *Dies iræ* movement. While neither G minor nor C minor, the two rivals for tonal control of the 'Dies iræ' section, is ever confirmed by a cadence within the section, the ambiguity is less pronounced after the strong statement of C minor in the preceding section of the *Libera me* movement. But if this passage were used as the opening of the *Dies iræ* movement, there would have been no context to ameliorate the ambiguity. Verdi's main concern in rewriting this passage was to increase tonal stability, but within the key of G minor rather than C minor, which was so strong in the original version. And yet the tonal ambiguity is preserved: Verdi was reluctant to use the straightforward and powerful method of providing a strong cadence in G minor. Instead, he opens the section with a statement of the G-minor triad and prolongs it for some

Ex. 9.2   1869 *Libera me*: bb. 42–6

twenty bars.[10] It is only this massive dose of the G-minor triad, followed shortly by an emphasis on its dominant (but as a minor triad), that forces us to accept it – *faute de mieux* – as the tonic. Any harmonic adventures at this point would have destroyed the effect, and so Verdi had to sacrifice the modulating theme of the 1869 version and this theme's foreshadowing of the fugue subject later in the movement. (Perhaps he compensated for the loss of the latter by giving the soprano a similar descending gesture in bb. 38–40.)

Although Verdi discarded the original version of the opening bars of the 'Dies iræ' section, with its adumbration of the fugue subject, he was able to incorporate one musical idea from it, though radically changing its function: the tenors' stepwise and generally chromatic ascent from the fifth degree to the tonic in the first three bars of Ex. 9.2 (1869: 42–4). In the final version this idea is no longer an inner voice subordinate to the main theme, however, but rather a sharply rhythmicized and strongly supported anacrusis to it (1874: 47–9). Not only has the line become more distinct, but it pushes more emphatically towards its destination because of the acceleration of harmonic rhythm (end of 1874: 48) and the cadential gesture. Furthermore, the goal of this chromatic ascent is based on an inversion of the motive borrowed from the tenor part of the 1869 movement.

After these thirty bars the 1874 version of the *Libera me* can once again be compared closely with the 1869 version. At this point Verdi reintroduces motivic material derived from the opening section: it will dominate the remainder of the section (a summary of these motivic connections is shown in Ex. 11.3). Bars 52–9, shown in Ex. 9.3, correspond to 1874: 75–83. In the

Ex. 9.3   *Libera me* 1869: bb. 52–9 / 1874: bb. 75–83

1869 version these eight bars consist of three legs of a sequence – each two bars long – and a final two-bar group. In the 1874 version these last two bars have been expanded into a violently syncopated three-bar group. This is another example of the technique of breaking off a well-established rhythmic or harmonic pattern in order to add weight to a point of arrival. In this case the extra bar cancels the pattern of two-bar iambic groups. The musical effect was clearly more important to Verdi than the declamation, which is better handled in the original version.

A brief transition leads to a sixteen-bar passage (1869: 66–91 / 1874: 90–105) based on another of the set of motives shown in Ex. 11.3. The passage descends nearly two octaves, rocking back and forth between g: V_7^9/iv and V_7^9 without resolution (this should recall the similar procedure at 1869: 27–30 / 1874: 28–32, although the earlier passage finally does cadence in C minor, the tonic), while making a diminuendo from *fortissimo* to *pianissimo*, then finally departs from the sixty-one-bar reprise of the opening of the 'Dies iræ music'

66

to return to the text and music of the lines 'Dum veneris judicare sæculum per ignem' (1869: 82–8 / 1874: 106–12) from the first section of the *Libera me* movement (cf. 1869 and 1874: 11–14). (The return is of course suggested by the liturgical text, as the verse concludes with a repetition of these lines from the opening of the responsory.) The return of the 'Dum veneris' brings little sense of return, as it emerges subtly out of the preceding passage. Not only is the motivic material created from the same mould, but the 'Dum veneris' passage begins as though it were to initiate a third statement of the basic eight-bar group. This much is true of both versions, but in 1874 Verdi weaved into the sixteen-bar passage three additional ideas from the 'Dum veneris': 1) the chromatic scale in the winds (bb. 91, 93, etc.), 2) the ⎣♪ ♪ figure in the brass, and 3) the choral exclamation 'Dies iræ'. Earlier we saw how by establishing then breaking a pattern, Verdi strengthened the articulation; the effect here is the converse: in order to undercut the sense of return or arrival, he momentarily continues the pattern. In effect, a thematic transformation is employed to undercut the effect of a literal return; the music continues until it is sharply cut off by the diminished-seventh chord shout at the end of the 'Dum veneris' passage.

The F, bass of this chord, suddenly collapses into quiet, mysterious octaves, momentarily non-committal about their harmonic function (1874: 115–16), then established as the dominant by inflections from both the lower and upper semitones and by a ♭VI–V progression in bleak parallel triads (bb. 119–20, 123–4). In the last seven bars, Verdi opens up a vast space between the sustained notes of oboe and horn and the anapestic figure in hollow open fifths of the bassoons, trombones, and low strings.[11]

Section III: 'Requiem æternam' (1869: 104–42; 1874: 132–70). Solo soprano and chorus, unaccompanied. 1869: A minor (ending in A major); Moderato, tornando al I. tempo, ₵ ($\quarternote$ = 72); 39 bars (*c.* 2'15"); 1874: B♭ minor (ending in B♭ major); Andante, ₵ ($\quarternote$ = 80); 39 bars (*c.* 2'00")

In the *Messa da Requiem* this is a reprise of text and music from the opening of the *Requiem*, but it was from this passage in the 1869 *Libera me* that Verdi fashioned the antiphon of the 'Requiem æternam', arranging it for strings with sporadic choral declamation. However, the Introit antiphon is significantly abbreviated: only approximately half of the section in the *Libera me* has a direct counterpart in the Introit. Even with the addition of the five-bar introductory phrase the 'Requiem æternam' antiphon totals twenty-seven bars for the first presentation (twenty-two for the reprise) against thirty-nine bars for the 'Requiem æternam' section of the *Libera me*. In the antiphon Verdi made no use of the fine passage leading into the *maggiore* section (1874 *Libera me*: 140–4), condensing it into two bars (*Requiem e Kyrie*, bb. 15–16), nor of the yet more beautiful final fifteen bars of the section. He may have felt that these passages – especially the pleading phrases at *Libera me* bb. 141–3 and the final four bars – would lose their effect if transferred to the orchestra. Furthermore, there was no disadvantage in reserving this material so that it would be new when it appeared in the reprise. Yet another consideration may have been the liturgically determined repetition of the antiphon after the Psalm verse. In the 1874 'Requiem æternam' the three sections – antiphon, verse, and repetition of the antiphon – are of approximately equal duration. Had Verdi incorporated the thirty-nine-bar passage from the *Libera me* in both statements of the antiphon, the outer sections would have dwarfed the verse, and might have made the 'Requiem æternam' too weighty to serve as an 'introduction' to the 'Kyrie'.

Both the 1869 version of this section and the opening of the *Requiem* are in A minor, but Verdi in revising the *Libera me* transposed the section to B♭ minor, with the reprise therefore returning a semitone above its initial appearance in the work.[12] This outcome is hardly astounding, for Verdi often presents recurring music a semitone above or below the initial statement, especially when one statement is primarily instrumental and the other vocal, as is the case here.[13] Various explanations for the transposition could be offered,[14] but whatever might be said about the effects of the revision, it is not unreasonable to suppose that Verdi's reasons for the transposition concerned the singers for whom the respective versions were written. There are, after all, documented instances as late as *Otello* where Verdi transposed numbers within his operas for the sake of vocal effect.[15] To write well for the voices, to use the sound of the human voice for musical effect, is an essential part of Verdi's art and craft.

Section IVa: Transition to the Fugue (1869: 143–8; 1874: 171–8). Soprano, chorus, and orchestra in 1869 version; soprano soloist and orchestra in 1874. 1869: Modulating to C minor; come prima [senza tempo] for two bars, then a tempo [Moderato], $\mathbf{C}$ ($\mathbf{\downarrow}$ = 72); 6 bars (*c*. 15"); 1874: Modulating to C minor; Senza misura for two bars, then Moderato, $\mathbf{C}$ ($\mathbf{\downarrow}$ = 100); 8 bars (*c*. 30"). The text consists of the first two lines only of the Respond (see p. 60).

The transition opens with a tremolo in the strings (b. 171), giving the soprano her pitch and a moment to catch her breath. She then enters with a recollection of her opening intonation.[16] Although the first four bars, with their prominent diminished-seventh chords, are tonally ambiguous, the purposeful ascent of the soprano's melodic line leads strongly to the g^2 and the *fortissimo* $^6_4$ chord, establishing C minor as the tonic. Her descending line (1874: 175–6) recalls her broad cadential phrase at the end of the first section (1874: 38–40) – and other concluding gestures sung by the female soloists – and foreshadows the fugue subject as well.

Section IV b: The Fugue. 1869: 149–391; 1874: 179–421. Fugue for chorus and orchestra, with important solo passages for the soprano soloist. C minor (ending in C major); Allegro risoluto, $\mathcal{C}$ ($\downarrow = 116$); 243 bars (*c.* 4'30"–5'00").[17] Orchestra: tutti. As prescribed by the liturgy, the text consists of a repetition of the Respond.

The fugue seems to have been considered the most problematic part of the entire work. Although some critics, Tovey and Toye among them, praised it warmly, Hanslick found it and the *Sanctus* to be 'conspicuous for their thematic insignificance and the stiffness and dryness of their development'.[18] Hussey found it difficult not to regret that the *Requiem* did not end with the reprise of the 'Requiem æternam'. 'The fugue may be admirable as a fugue [. . .], but its movement has always seemed too jaunty and its style too trivial to make it a satisfactory coping stone to the great edifice.' About its affect, this usually sensitive critic goes far astray: 'It is, indeed, customary for military bands returning from a funeral to relieve their feelings after the mournful business is over with gay marches, and Verdi may have felt that something cheerful would be an appropriate last thought to leave in the minds of a congregation gathered to do honour to that great comedian, Rossini.' Toye's characterization is closer to the mark; he views the fugue as 'so dynamic and insistent that one seems to sense the clamour of a multitude intent on achieving salvation by violence'.

When Verdi composed the *Libera me* in 1869, the fugue doubtless cost him more labour than the other sections, and when he re-examined it in 1874 he found that the effort expended on the fugue five years earlier obviated any substantial revision. There are comparatively few changes there, and with many of these the 1869 reading was copied into the 1874 autograph score and only later retouched. Each bar of the final version can be compared to a corresponding bar in the original.

Verdi's approach to this fugue is similar to that seen in the *Sanctus* fugue. There are three principal sections:

I. 179–206 (28 bb.) A 'normal' fugal exposition, with countersubjects, in the tonic key.

II. 207–311 (105 bb.) A middle section, marked by features associated with 'development': modulation, avoidance of the tonic, relative irregularity of phrase structure, and increased contrapuntal complexity (achieved in this case by stretto). As in the *Sanctus*, there is an expressive, *dolcissimo* augmentation of the main theme; rather than marking the return to the tonic and the beginning of the third section, however, in the *Libera me* it appears shortly before the 'retransition', that is, before the extensive dominant preparation for the corresponding tonal return.

III. 312–421 (110 bb.). A return to the tonic, with a simplification of the phrase structure and of the texture, beginning with stretto but ending with homophony.

After the exposition the complete fugue subject is heard but once (bb. 239–46); it is at other times represented by its head motive (or, on one occasion, its conclusion), presented in regular, inverted, or augmented form. The fugue is dominated by the subject (whether complete or abbreviated): except for a short episode (and its repetition) it is virtually always present. Furthermore, the countersubjects from the exposition are thereafter forgotten.

Exposition. The angular subject is patently an inversion of the principal subject of the *Sanctus* fugue, and the ii^7 chord with which the subject begins may also recall the ii$^4_2$ chord at the opening of the *Libera me*. The subject is asymmetrically structured: $2 + 3 + 2 + 1$, the last bar eliding with the next statement. Tovey comments, 'Classical practice is not in favour of full closes in fugal expositions, but Verdi likes them well enough to mark them with the full orchestra.'[19] The order in which the voices enter – A S B T – is unusual but logical. Considerations of range limit the subject form to A and B, the answer to S and T. Since B S A T and A T B S are problematic (because of overly wide spacing and avoidance of awkward voice crossing, respectively), only B T A S and A S B T are viable. Of these, only the latter allowed Verdi to employ invertible counterpoint: note the effective combination between the fifth and sixth bars, alternating between outward-expanding and inward-contracting motion between the subject and first countersubject.

Middle section. After the exposition the process of abbreviating the subject begins with an inversion of the subject's first nine notes, the inversion clinching the subject's relationship to the principal subject of the *Sanctus* (bb. 207–11). The episode that follows (bb. 213–18) lacks significant connections with the subject or with the countersubjects, although it may recall the most important family of themes in the *Libera me* (see Ex. 11.3).

The next stage (bb. 219–32) is a quiet plateau, again based on a nine-note version of the subject, presented in both regular and inverted forms. At the return to a *fortissimo* dynamic level (bb. 233–8) the condensation of the subject continues: it is pared down to its first six notes and re-rhythmicized ♩ ♪♩♩ | ♩ ♩ . This will remain one of the two important versions of the subject until well into the third section of the fugue, when it will be supplanted by an even shorter version. At bb. 253–61 Verdi introduces the stretto texture so prevalent in the final section of the fugue. The contraltos, doubled by solo trumpet, dominate a transition passage using the six-note version of the subject, now presented *dolcissimo*.

Thus far in the fugue the soprano soloist has remained silent, but at bb. 262–76 she emerges with an *espressivo*, *dolcissimo* statement – in augmentation – of a further abbreviation of the subject, now of the first five notes of the theme.[20] The following passage recalls a technique seen earlier in the movement, that of underarticulating an arrival by working its salient material into the preceding passage. In the 1869 version the soloist rejoins the sopranos of the chorus immediately after the augmentation passage (i.e., at 1869: 246), but in the 1874 version she retains her independence for eight additional bars (1874: 276–83) before her part merges with the chorus at the reprise of the episode heard earlier (cf. bb. 213ff. and 284ff.). Her part in these eight bars consists of the repeated-note motive of the episode, with the effect that the soprano seems to propose the motive and to convince the chorus to take it up with her. After another partial statement of the subject (now represented by the fourth to seventh bars, rather than the opening – bb. 290–3) and an ingenious sequence in stretto, a half cadence and pause clearly mark the end of the middle section of the fugue.

Final section. The remainder of the fugue emphasizes features associated with closure. It remains solidly in the tonic key, and tends to unfold in more regular, easily scanned phrase structure. The texture becomes less dense towards the end, after beginning with a series of strettos. While in the *Sanctus* the entire final section was homophonic, here the move to a lighter texture is more gradual and less complete. The soloist, who first emerged about midway through the middle section, comes to dominate the final section, especially in the 1874 version.[21]

This final section opens with a pair of symmetrical eight-bar strettos, with the voices entering in every bar, alternating between subject and answer forms. In the next pair of strettos, a canon with the subject now presented at two-bar intervals, the soprano soloist re-emerges, overlaying a countermelody above. Verdi copied into the 1874 autograph the 1869 version of her line, with its ungainly descent through an eleventh (see Ex. 9.4), but subsequently

Ex. 9.4   Soprano part of 1869 *Libera me*: bb. 299–306

fashioned it into a declamatory outburst, emphasizing the dominant and providing the decisive reversal of direction that the line had lacked, as well as providing greater continuity by the tie spanning the second and third bars (at the expense of the declamation, however).[22] After the two pairs of strettos, a sequence on the six-note version of the subject leads to another weighty – though *ppp* – half cadence, another significant demarcation.

Beginning with 1869: 321 / 1874: 351 there is an eight-bar dialogue between the fugue subject, finally pared down to four notes, and a descending four-note motive, with a dominant pedal between them; the passage is repeated an octave lower. The four-note motive derives from the soprano's countermelody at 1869: 299–300 / 1874: 329–30; the relationship, perfectly clear in the 1869 version, was obscured somewhat by Verdi's revision of the countermelody. The dialogue is built upon a stepwise descending sequence – but unlike other uses of this procedure,[23] it is now controlled by the dominant pedal, a sign of the directionality associated with closure. The fugal texture is radically simplified: yet another sign of closure.

The preparation for the climax is based on an obsessively repeating motive in the basses, in which the rhythm of the first bar of the fugue subject is superimposed upon the F–E♭–D contour of the soprano's countermelody (and perhaps also the descending third motive from the 'Dies iræ music' and elsewhere – see Ex. 11.3e). This is shaped into a sequence that, unlike the usual pattern, climbs rather than wilting downward, accelerating from four-bar segments to two-bar segments, then broadening to a three-bar segment at the end. At the *tutta forza* the motive is expanded to return to its starting-point (Ex. 11.3f). The climax of the fugue is similar in the two versions, but in the 1869 version the line halts at b♭[2] and the solo soprano is a mere chorister (see Ex. 9.5). In the 1874 version she breaks free from the chorus and carries the line up to c[3], the first and last in the movement, and only the second in the entire *Requiem*. At 1874: 394 it is harmonized as the 7 in ii[7], not only a more pungent sound than the V/iv of the 1869 version, but also the chord that generates the fugue subject. Indeed, the soprano sweeps down through the first four notes of the subject, all that remain of it, in augmentation.

Ex. 9.5   1869 *Libera me*, bb. 352–70 (chorus)

The final stretch of the movement (1869: 371–91 / 1874: 401–21) consists of two final statements of the dialogue that was interrupted by the climactic passage just discussed, but now stabilized with a tonic (rather than dominant) pedal and adjusted to end on the tonic major chord. Verdi had originally entrusted the last unmeasured declamation to the basses, but in the 1874 version there is a final change in favour of the soloist: the soprano is allowed to end the movement, just as she had begun it.

What are we to make of the turn to C major at the end (bb. 408 and 416–21)? Noting that C major is the key of the *Agnus Dei*, John Roeder associates the resolution with 'the Lamb of God, who takes away the sins of the world' and concludes that the sinner has found redemption.[24] But if the turn from C minor to major soon after the soprano has sung a climactic high c^3 evokes an earlier moment in the work, it is surely the climax of the 'Rex tremendæ majestatis'. Note the textual parallelism – 'salva me' and 'libera me' – and recall Verdi's comment linking the two 'phrases where a high c is sustained at length', passages which made such an effect in Paris (see p. 15). Although the 'Rex tremendæ' ends in an optimistic vein, much has happened since then, and there is no more assurance that its plea for mercy will be granted. In any case, it is doubtful that any reference to an earlier section – whether the *Agnus Dei*, the 'Rex tremendæ', or any other – can overshadow the impression made by this passage in its immediate context and its clear depiction of the prayer of a terrified supplicant, murmured by the soprano in her low register, inevitably producing a *voce cupa* effect. As for the turn to C major, 'there is no subsequent lightening of the gloom, no winding up in a triumphant C major. The E natural that marks the repeated final cadences has the quality of a *tierce de Picardie* . . . '.[25] Nothing has changed; the soprano is no more certain of the outcome now than at the beginning of the movement.

Few of the early critics considered the question of the work's optimism or pessimism, but Reyer's description of the last bars as 'la dernière lueur de la lampe qui s'éteint sous les arceaux d'une cathédrale' is on the mark.[26] And in this century Toye, who sensed in the fugue 'the clamour of a multitude intent on achieving salvation by violence', writes of the end: 'Force has failed; only the appeal to mercy remains, now so abject that it is spoken rather than sung.' One thinks of Verdi's *Stabat Mater* and *Te Deum*, which reach resounding, affirmative climaxes and then deflate them, falling into doubt and despair.[27]

Perhaps Ernest Newman's comments about the *Missa solemnis* apply even more strongly to Verdi's *Requiem*: 'The conclusion of it all is enigmatic . . . Does [the composer] really believe that the prayer will be answered, or does he leave it all as a kind of question mark projected upon the remote, indifferent sky?'[28]

10

Two revisions

The 'Liber scriptus' rewritten

As we have seen, in May 1875 Verdi replaced the original setting of the 'Liber scriptus' section of the *Dies iræ* – a fugue for chorus and orchestra – with the mezzo-soprano solo performed ever since.[1] Why did he find the original setting wanting? We need not enquire into the defects of this fugue, as Verdi did not try to improve it but simply replaced it with a piece of a very different type. I doubt that his decision was influenced by the few critics who did not find the fugue effective or appropriate,[2] and it is unlikely that he had somehow discovered and been troubled by the resemblance of the fugue subject to that of the second *Kyrie* of Donizetti's Requiem, premiered and published in 1870. To discover why Verdi decided to replace the piece, we must consider it in its context.

One clue comes from the letter of early April 1874 in which Verdi responds to one of Ricordi's queries about the first shipment of the *Requiem* score: ' . . . the transition from A to G minor is very ugly, but more in theory than in practice. It would be easy to prepare it with a simple chord, but I prefer it as it is.' The 'Mors stupebit' builds powerful dominant preparation for a cadence in D minor that, in the first version, never happens: the 'Liber scriptus' fugue instead races off in G minor, leaving the preceding section hanging on its dominant, and thus in a movement where sections are otherwise cogently linked, makes the 'Liber scriptus' seem a new independent piece. The 1875 version remedies this problem in a very direct way: remaining in D minor, it grows out of and further prolongs the dominant that ends the 'Mors stupebit', then finally supplies the long-awaited strong authentic cadence. But the relationship of the 'Liber scriptus' to the reprise of the 'Dies iræ' music that follows it is even more important.

The fugal setting of the 'Liber scriptus', by anticipating the character and salient features of the following reprise, undercuts its effect. The fugue anticipates the G-minor tonality of the 'Dies iræ', its use of chorus, and nearly

75

its tempo (fugue: $\downarrow$ = 144; 'Dies iræ': $\downarrow$ = 80). The 1875 solo version provides the needed contrast: when the reprise arrives, both its tonality and its use of chorus is new (we can neglect the background muttering of the chorus in the 'Liber scriptus'), and its tempo is nearly double that of the preceding section ('Liber scriptus': $\downarrow$ = 88; reprise: $\downarrow$ = 80).

The operatic origins of the 'Lacrymosa'

The 'Lacrymosa' is dominated by its opening melody, which Tovey characterized as 'naive enough for *Il Trovatore*'. He was on the right track: the 'Lacrymosa' melody does indeed have its origins in the opera house. As we have seen, it stems from a duet Verdi composed for *Don Carlos* in 1866 but discarded even before the first orchestral rehearsal.[3] And yet one would want to take issue with the word 'naive'. Comparing some aspects of this melody with its model sets in high relief some of its subtleties. Ex. 10.1 presents the two versions of the theme, along with a reduction of the accompaniment. The bass line is *coll' 8va bassa*, and the added figures indicate the prevailing chord in each half-bar – in some bars these chords are not sounded until the offbeat.

Some of the revisions of the melody are obviously due to the differences in the metric structure of the two poems: for example, since each line of the 'Lacrymosa' text has an accent on the penultimate rather than the final syllable, Verdi naturally ended most phrases with a metrically weak cadence on the second beat of a bar rather than on the downbeat. In the final phrase, however, wanting a strong cadence ending on the downbeat, he set the penultimate, accented syllable to a long note, a standard procedure throughout the *Dies iræ* (see p. 24). It should be emphasized, however, that the scope of the revisions extends well beyond those required merely in order to adapt the original melody to the new, Latin text. (Moreover, even those revisions determined by considerations of declamation bring other, serendipitous advantages as well, as will be seen.)

Although the text of the 'Lacrymosa' is more symmetrical than that of the duet, there is a far greater variety of rhythmic figures than in the duet, with its eight presentations of the same rhythmic pattern – $\flat$ ⌠⌠⌠ | ⌠ – or an obvious equivalent. In the original version, the relentless repetition of the rhythmic pattern, often reinforced by the recurrence of the opening melodic motive (or its inversion, as in bb. 4–5), tends to segment the melody into one-bar units, an effect aggravated by the strong profile of the rhythmic motive itself. While in the duet the five-note figure is unequivocally an anacrusis

Ex. 10.1   The themes of the *Don Carlos* duet and the 'Lacrymosa' compared

slamming into the downbeat, the corresponding figure in the 'Lacrymosa' is somewhat ambiguous: it can serve as downbeat almost as well as upbeat. Verdi takes advantage of this ambiguity later in the 'Lacrymosa' when he passes this motive through the voices at half-bar intervals (bb. 657–60).

The catchwords 'unity' and 'continuity' are often used as though they were synonyms, but in the duet theme the 'unifying' rhythmic and melodic motives create a sense of *dis*continuity. Verdi ameliorated the hectic stop-and-start effect present in the original version, especially in the first half of the theme. One reason for this lack of continuity has already been mentioned, but the main cause is the decisive cadences in bb. 3 and 5. In the 'Lacrymosa' these cadences are weakened, and each phrase is linked with the following one. In bb. 2–3, the final version of the melodic line avoids the leading tone and leaps to the tonic from the dissonant d$\flat^1$ rather than from a tone within the dominant triad itself. Instead of sustaining or repeating the tonic, the line merely passes through it on its way to the dominant. Not only does this de-emphasize the cadence, but it provides a useful melodic link to the next phrase, which picks up the same f. The effect of continuity is also fostered by the metrically weak phrase-endings discussed above.

In the second phrase, the first version lunges immediately to V/III, beginning a very forceful cadence in III (III: V$^{6-5}_{4-3}$–I, with octave leap in the bass) which takes up most of the phrase. The melody forces its way down the dominant seventh chord (of III) to land solidly on the root of the D$\flat$ triad. This cadence is almost as decisive as the one at the end of the theme, and it severs the theme in two. In the 'Lacrymosa' the move to III is far smoother (note the G$\flat$ triad, which connects the realms of i and III), and the strong cadential bass line of the duet is replaced with a line that unobtrusively passes through the d$\flat$ on its way to the B$\flat$ in b. 6, spanning and linking the two phrases. The vocal line avoids the d$\flat$ entirely, settling for the less stable third of the chord – the f, which once again provides a link with the following phrase.

In the final phrase (from the second half of b. 7) a decisive cadence is finally in order. Thus far the duet has overemphasized its cadences, but now it misses its chance. The final phrase presents two more statements of the rhythmic motive, with a caesura on the tonic that checks the drive to the cadence in mid-passage and breaks the line into two groups in different registers, thus reinforcing the disjunctive effect of the caesura separating them. Note too that the final approach to the tonic is from $\hat{3}$ – the same technique used to *soften* the first cadence in the 'Lacrymosa'.

Thus far in the 'Lacrymosa' the slower values tend to be placed on the first half of the bar, while the second half usually consists of an anacrusis of eighth-notes. In the penultimate bar Verdi reverses this pattern. Now the eighth-note motion occurs at the beginning of the bar, continuing the sweep begun in the previous bar; then the half-note brakes in preparation for the cadence. The broadening of the phrase rhythm from one bar to two bars presents a higher-level analogy to the broadening within the penultimate bar itself. Here there is the sense of culmination lacking in the duet. In the 'Lacrymosa' the descent to $\hat{1}$ is immediately balanced by the stepwise ascent from $\hat{3}$ to $\hat{5}$ – appropriately picking up once more the f that played such an important role in the first half of the theme. The reversal of direction pulls the two registers together into an implied two-part contrapuntal structure later made explicit in the 'Lacrymosa' (for two different realizations, see bb. 663–5, Trombones II and III; soprano and basses). In the cadence the downward fifth leap has the forcefulness required, and, thanks to the alterations earlier in the theme, there are no cadences that rival it in strength.

11

The unità musicale *of the* Requiem

'The composition (however good the individual numbers may be) will necessarily lack *unità musicale*', Verdi wrote in his letter proposing the *Messa per Rossini*. Earlier that year he had rehearsed the shortcomings of *primo ottocento* opera, regretting 'above all, the lack of that golden thread that connects every part and constitutes – rather than unconnected, individual pieces [*pezzi incoerenti*] – an *opera in musica*'.[1] And nearly fifteen years earlier he had expressed his belief 'that you can make twenty pieces of good music that make a bad work when put together. A work composed by many composers, even if they are all geniuses, will always turn out without unity, without character, without style, and above all, there won't be a principal idea that reigns over and dominates the whole composition.'[2]

In the *Requiem* the most obvious source of coherence – let us choose that translation of '*unità*' rather than the more militant 'unity' – comes from the system of reprises of the 'Requiem æternam' and the 'Dies iræ'. The reappearance in the final movement of music heard earlier is not only a common procedure in nineteenth-century music in general but also has precedents in other Requiems, including the Requiems of Michael Haydn, Paisiello, Mozart/Süssmayr, and Berlioz.[3] The function of the reprises is not merely to impart coherence, however, as they also have consequences for the expressive plot of the work. The 'Dies iræ' music appears four times in the course of the *Requiem*: three times in the *Dies iræ* – where it serves to articulate the changes in 'voice' (see p. 24 on the reprises' function within the *Dies iræ*) – and once in the *Libera me*. The liturgical 'Libera me' text gives equal weight to the two central images of the Requiem Mass, 'dies iræ' and 'requiem æternam', and the *Libera me* of Verdi's *Requiem* treats them more or less symmetrically, allotting them nearly the same amount of actual time. However, the emphasis placed on 'dies iræ' through the system of reprises in the *Dies iræ* movement makes that image, rather than 'requiem æternam', the 'principal idea that reigns over and dominates the whole composition'.

In addition to these reprises of the 'Requiem æternam' and 'Dies iræ' music, there are also more subtle thematic connections weaving through the *Requiem* as a whole. I have already discussed Verdi's use of thematic transformation within the 'Kyrie', 'Rex tremendæ', 'Ingemisco', and the two fugues; now we turn to thematic connections spanning more than a single movement. A number of the important themes of the work belong to one of two families. The first family is characterized by descending disjunct motion through a ninth or larger interval (e.g., the *Libera me* fugue subject). The bold descending gestures by the female soloists constitute an important subgroup. In addition to the immediate family shown in Ex. 11.1, we must recognize an extended family that includes themes that are related to one or more of the members of the immediate family, while lacking at least some of its defining characteristics: although the *Sanctus* fugue subject outlines an octave and ascends, its close relationship to the *Libera me* fugue subject warrants its inclusion in the extended family. Similarly the opening theme of the *Requiem* is soon transformed into Ex. 11.1a.

The second family is characterized by conjunct motion through a third or fourth followed by a return to the starting-point, either by conjunct motion or by leap. Ex. 11.2 shows the immediate family, while Ex. 11.3 presents six related examples from the *Libera me*.

Even accompanimental figures may serve as recurring themes. Five sections of the *Dies iræ* and the 'Hostias' of the *Offertorio* are linked by isolated notes inflected by a grace-note a semitone below, most typically played by winds, and usually appearing on offbeats.[4] That this figure (or any other recurring element discussed here) may appear in other works as well does not disqualify it from serving as a link within the *Requiem*. That is, when we listen to the 'Hostias' the figure should evoke the similar passages in the *Dies Iræ* – whether or not it may also evoke Philippe's aria in *Don Carlos*.

The most direct way to associate one passage with another is through thematic recall, but other means are available as well. The endings of the *Requiem e Kyrie*, *Dies iræ*, and *Lux æterna* movements are linked by gestures of harmonic mystification. The connection between the *Dies iræ* and the *Lux æterna* is especially strong: both passages are in B♭ major, and the harmonic quirk consists of an interpolation of a third-related chord (III or VI, rather than the 'normal' minor triad belonging to the major mode). At the end of both movements the range rapidly contracts to repeated low-lying *pianissimo*

Ex. 11.1

(a) *Requiem e Kyrie*, bb. 17–20

(b) *Dies iræ*, bb. 226–9 ('Liber scriptus')

(c) *Dies iræ*, bb. 280–4 ('Quid sum miser')

(d) *Dies iræ*, bb. 322–4 ('Rex tremendæ')

(e) *Libera me*, bb. 36–40

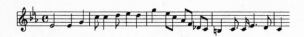

(f) *Libera me*, bb. 179–86

Ex. 11.2

(a)   *Requiem e Kyrie*, bb. 28–9 ('Te decet hymnus')

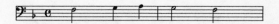

(b)   *Dies iræ*, bb. 3–9

(c)   *Dies iræ*, bb. 457–60 ('Ingemisco')

(d)   *Dies iræ*, bb. 511–13 ('Confutatis')

(e)   *Dies iræ*, bb. 625–7 ('Lacrymosa')

Ex. 11.2   (continued)

(f) *Offertorio*, bb. 120–5 ('Hostias')

(g)   *Agnus Dei*, bb. 1–4

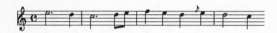

(h)   *Lux æterna*, bb. 15–19

(i)   *Lux æterna*, bb. 54–6

chords with the third as the highest note. Another movement, the *Libera me*, lacks the harmonic twist at its close, but the spacing of the final tonic major chords, with the third on top, suffices to connect it with the other two passages, especially with the *Dies iræ*. And of course vocal sonority can also connect passages, for example, those in which the soprano climbs to a high c^3 (see pp. 73–4).

Another recurring element is tempo; this is especially clear in the two cases

Ex. 11.3   Related themes within the *Libera me*

(a)   bb. 75–6

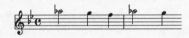

(b)   bb. 90–1

(c)   bb. 106–7

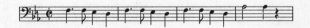

(d)   bb. 138–41

(e)   bb. 367–70

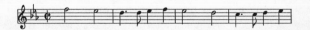

(f)   bb. 382–5

where adjacent sections share *lo stesso movimento*: the 'Rex tremendæ majestatis' and 'Recordare' ($\downarrow = 72$), and the reprises of the 'Requiem æternam' and 'Dies iræ' within the *Libera me* ($\downarrow$, then $\downarrow = 80$).[5] In two instances the same tempo recurs after a single intervening section: in the opening and closing sections of the *Offertorio* and the 'Hostias' ($66 = \downarrow$ and $\downarrow$, respectively), and the 'Tuba mirum' and 'Liber scriptus' ($\downarrow = 88$).[6]

The most controversial analytical issue, as always, is the role of tonality. The *Requiem* is not in a single key, nor is there any tonal design spanning the entire work. Indeed, Verdi's *Requiem* has a looser tonal structure than its predecessors. The Requiems of Mozart, Cherubini, and Berlioz begin and end with the same tonic, and the *Messa per Rossini* at least places the opening movement in the dominant (G minor) of the key (C minor) of the movement that follows (*Dies iræ*) and of the final movement (*Libera me*). Moreover, the *Messa per Rossini* committee was keen on providing an overall tonal structure for the *Dies iræ*: not only does the movement begin and end in C minor – similarly, the *Dies iræ* settings of Mozart, Cherubini, and Berlioz have tonal closure – but it also concludes with a strongly directed circle of fifths leading from the 'Ingemisco' to the end: a–D–G–c.

To be sure, Verdi's *Dies iræ* is not wholly lacking in 'teleological' tonality: from the 'Mors stupebit', which provides dominant preparation for the D-minor 'Liber scriptus', to the F-major 'Recordare' it moves through a descending circle of fifths (though with modal mixture), and the 'Quid sum miser' returns to cadence in the G minor heard at the opening of the movement; however, it contains the only authentic cadences in G in the entire *Requiem*. But on the whole Verdi seems little interested in the committee's grand tonal plans. His *Dies iræ* movement begins in G minor and ends with the B♭ minor/major of the 'Lacrymosa', a key not previously heard.[7]

Even if there is no overall tonal progression governing the *Requiem*, it could be argued that the recurrence of particular keys (e.g., B♭ minor) or tonal relationships (e.g., ♭VI of the reigning key) – like the recurrence of any recognizable element – could serve to impart *unità musicale*. Four keys – C (major and minor), B♭ (major and minor), F major and G minor – are established as tonic in three or more places in the *Requiem*, and on two occasions statements of the G-minor 'Dies iræ' music lead to B♭ minor (to the 'Lacrymosa' and to the 'Requiem æternam' section within the *Libera me*). Moreover, there is a prominent alternation of C and B♭ in the last three movements. The significance of such tonal recurrences will vary from one listener to another, but it is clear that their significance is increased when supported by the simultaneous recurrence of other elements. In the *Requiem* the best example is the series of reprises of the 'Dies iræ' music, invariably occurring in G minor – although it would be perverse to claim that what the listener perceives is primarily a return of key rather than theme. Similarly, that the G♭-major passages in the 'Lacrymosa' and *Lux æterna* are both scored for unaccompanied solo voices makes the tonal connection more evident. (Here the tonal connection is twofold, as in both cases the G♭ is ♭VI of the governing key.) The similar themes of the 'Hostias' and *Agnus Dei* are both in C major (but the main theme of the 'Ingemisco', also similar, is not). But there are just as many cases where the tonal return is not supported by the return of theme, texture, or other elements. It would be hard to argue that the shared F-major tonality succeeds in linking the vastly dissimilar 'Te decet hymnus', 'Recordare', and *Sanctus* in any significant way. That is, most listeners will probably connect, for example, the 'Te decet hymnus' more with other passages evoking the *stile antico* than to the *Sanctus*. Style too can be a recurring pattern.

Continuity is a related question. It is generally accepted that a greater continuity between sections is a hallmark of Verdi's late style. This is certainly the case within the *Dies iræ* movement, in which the constituent sections either lack tonal closure or are joined to the following section by a transition.[8] But Verdi's procedure between *movements* is very different: here he tends to favour disjunction. Even though three of the movements – including the final one – end with the third in the uppermost voice, none of them can be said to lack solid closure or to leave tensions to be resolved by the following movement. Nor are there links of tempo or harmonic progression that bind adjacent pairs of movements together. In four of the six pairs, the new movement begins a major second away from the final chord of the preceding one, therefore without any common tones.[9]

While *unità musicale* is a consistent strand in Verdi's thought, he never explained what he meant by it or what characteristics a work would need to possess it. I doubt that he had in mind an 'organic unity' that places every passage into a hierarchy or network, that derives everything from 'germinating cells', or regards every passage as part of an all-encompassing teleological tonal or linear progression. At any rate, analysts who attempt to deal with his works in that way are likely to be disappointed.[10] Verdi's *unità musicale* is less like that of a Bach fugue or a Webern serial composition than that of a rondo, although a rondo with many recurring ideas: certain moments in the work are linked by these recurring ideas, while other moments are not drawn into any overarching design. However, these recurring ideas are not restricted to thematic material, but, as we have seen, may also include texture, harmonic progressions, orchestration, tempos, and the like. Furthermore, in music with text – be it an opera, song cycle, or liturgical work – the text contributes its own measure of coherence, or, expressed differently, reduces the importance of a coherence based solely on musical values. Verdi's *Requiem* has, I think, all the *unità musicale* that it needs.

12

A question of genre

In his book on the *Missa solemnis* William Drabkin, after noting the importance of musical qualities that can be understood independently of the text, rightly warns, 'Of course, it would be a mistake to suppose that these musical features manifest themselves in the same way here as in, say, a sonata or symphony.'[1] That is also true of the *Requiem*, of course, but confusion over the work's genre has come from the other direction: that of regarding the work as an unstaged opera. For the *Requiem* lies somewhere between the poles of opera and symphony. At times the music traces its own expressive plot virtually unaided by the text; this is especially true where the text is brief and lacks sharp mood swings (e.g., 'Kyrie', 'Quid sum miser', and *Agnus Dei*). But at other times Verdi is acutely attentive to shifting images in the text, even to the point of depicting individual words: 'Quantus *tremor* est futurus', for example (see p. 26). And at times the individual singers assume the role of characters, almost as in opera, before retreating into anonymity.

Is the *Requiem* 'good church music'?

Far more than any issue about the musical value of the work, the complex of issues around the work's genre (including its suitability as church music and the composer's 'sincerity') have dominated the reception of the *Requiem* from the very beginning. The question of whether the work was 'operatic' is central to the controversy, as most writers believed that, if it were so, it could not be good church music (or even good religious music). And so, critics favourable to the work took pains to establish that, while the *Requiem* might be 'dramatic', it is not 'operatic' or 'theatrical'. And one of the most damning things Hans von Bülow could find to say about the work was to characterize it as 'Oper im Kirchengewande' (see p. 12). Von Bülow was, of course, predisposed to loathe the work, but Frederick J. Crowest, a strong supporter of Verdi, praised the work as 'one of the scores that . . . will best preserve Verdi's name', but then dismissed it as 'not great sacred music'.[2] The 'abundant theoretical workmanship . . . has not enabled Verdi to rid himself of . . . characteristics which stamp southern musical art as plainly as they do the architecture and the person. Sensuous and exciting music is acceptable enough in its way, but it does not constitute good Church music.' This is genre criticism run amok, and his comments on national characteristics also make one slightly uneasy nowadays.

In this century, Francis Toye, acknowledging the difficulty of advocating a work written 'in a style rejected in this country [England] by Anglicans and Catholics alike', finessed the problem by redefining the genre of the work, thus changing its dramatic nature from a liability to an asset: 'Perhaps the best way for an Anglo-Saxon to approach the [*Requiem*] is to think of it as a kind of oratorio, a sacred opera if you will, on the subject of the Last Judgment, with Alessandro Manzoni's soul as the objective theme of the drama.'[3]

Clearly the *Requiem* can be made to function as liturgical music: it was first performed in church as part of a religious ceremony and, compared to Berlioz's *Grande messe des morts*, Verdi's departures from the liturgical text are negligible. As we have seen, however, in the five years following the premiere, Verdi would direct one or more performances on seven different occasions, but never again as part of a liturgical ceremony or in church.[4] As Eduard Hanslick put it, 'In the concert halls of Paris, London, and Vienna, he introduced it to the congregation for which it was really intended – the musical community.'[5] Hanslick argues that suitability for the church is no longer a valid criterion for sacred music:

In regard to sacred music we tend nowadays to listen to and appraise it as art. What the church finds in it to praise or blame is a matter of indifference. . . . We children of our time . . . see in the *Stabat Mater*, the Requiem, even in the text of the Mass, a poem hallowed by content and tradition, but still a poem at the service of the composer as material for his work. What he makes of it is, for us, a work of free art, whose right to exist is embodied in its own artistic greatness and beauty, not in its usefulness to the church. In a word, we think of the concert hall rather than the church, and so do the masters.[6]

Verdi probably would have agreed. He had expressed his concerns about the lack of unity of the *Messa per Rossini* – an aesthetic judgment – but he seems not to have worried about its status (or that of the *Requiem*) as church music or about its religious spirit. 'Can our *Mass* [the *Messa per Rossini*] stand comparison with the two works of Rossini?' he asked the Committee. 'I'm not talking here about their religious character, or of the contrapuntal skill of those fugues. Let anyone believe who wants to. I'm a bit of an atheist in this, but I do believe in the musical value of those two compositions.'[7]

Leaving the matter to individual consciences seems the best course here as well: whether listeners find Verdi's *Requiem* to be 'good Church music' may depend less upon their view of the work than on their notions about the proper role for music in the church. The question of the work's suitability as religious music has been carried by some critics into the issue of sincerity and Verdi's religious beliefs. Hanslick would have had no patience for such investigations: 'The subjective religiousness of the artist must be left out of the question; criticism is not inquisition. At the same time, a composer's faith is no guarantee for the religious dignity of the work, and vice versa.'[8]

The sincerity question inevitably leads back to the question of genre. According to one music history textbook, Verdi's *Requiem* is 'operatic in form and style, but profoundly sincere' – that little word 'but' speaks volumes.[9] And who has not heard the tired half-witticism that 'the *Requiem* is Verdi's greatest opera'? Verdi would have objected to this: he clearly wanted to distance the *Requiem* from opera.[10] But rather than challenging Hans von Bülow's contemptuous characterization of the *Requiem* as an 'Oper im Kirchengewande', many writers on Verdi have accepted it – together with its implicit anti-operatic bias – but attempted to twist it into evidence of Verdi's sincerity.[11] Verdi was sincere in adopting his own (operatic) style, the argument runs, rather than aping someone else's (presumably Palestrina's). This seems to be one of the principal strands of Giuseppina Verdi's oft-cited statement:

They have spoken much about whether the spirit of this sacred music is more or less religious, about not having followed the idea [*idea tipo*] of Mozart, of Cherubini, etc. etc. I say that a man like Verdi must write like Verdi, that is, according to his way of feeling and interpreting the texts. Then too, if the religions have a beginning, a development, modifications or transformations, etc. according to the times and according to the people, clearly the religious spirit and the works that express it must carry the imprint of the time, and, if you will, of the individual. I would have, so to speak, rejected a *Messa* of Verdi, that was made according to the model of A, B, or C.[12]

As a defence of Verdi's sincerity this is not entirely satisfactory, for it would therefore follow that historicist works like Verdi's *Pater noster* (1880) – 'written for five voices without accompaniment in the Palestrina style, but naturally with modern modulations and harmony' – would be insincere.[13] Surely the examples of Picasso and Stravinsky should show the futility of assigning grades for sincerity according to the style of the composition. Indeed, it is questionable whether the artist's 'sincerity' is a useful criterion for works of art at all.

Is the *Requiem* 'operatic'?

In any event, many writers have been so concerned with defending Verdi's sincerity that they have failed to note the wide gulf that separates the *Requiem* from Verdi's operatic works.[14] Is the *Requiem* 'operatic'? And if not, is it at least 'dramatic'? The *Requiem* can surely be called 'dramatic' in the metaphorical sense of 'forcefully effective', but it would be difficult to consider it 'dramatic' in the more central and restricted sense of resembling a literary drama. It obviously lacks some important characteristics generally found in dramatic genres: a plot encompassing the entire work, a correspondence between each character and a singer assigned to the role, and characters who interact with each other. (Furthermore, unlike opera, it is not staged.) All this has consequences for the musical setting. Since there is no plot, Verdi had a free hand in deploying his forces, and could have a quartet or a chorus whenever he wanted, without worrying about bringing characters on-stage and then leading them off again. None of Verdi's operas has as many quartets – four (including one at the opening of the work, before operatic principals could be properly introduced) – or places such heavy responsibilities upon the chorus, both from the amount of participation and the difficulties (since the chorus needed neither to memorize its music nor to engage in stage action).

Furthermore, the *Requiem* lacks the dichotomy between text that unfolds in something approaching 'real time' (e.g., a recitative) and that which unfolds in 'suspended' or 'frozen' time (e.g., a reflective set-piece). Nor do we have the sense of an alternation between passages that privilege the text (e.g., recitative) and others that privilege the music (e.g., set-pieces). There are a few passages of declamatory writing in the *Requiem*, but almost nothing that could be mistaken for an operatic recitative, apart from several brief passages of monotone declamation (of which, more later). And there is little use of *parlante*, where the orchestra is entrusted with the musical continuity (often clear-cut instrumental melodies), the voices merely fitting in their parts against the orchestral melody. *Parlante* has often been considered a progressive feature, a way of moving the action forward in real time (as opposed to lyric numbers) while retaining musical expressivity and cohesion not available through recitative. Verdi seems to have valued it as a useful solution to a problem of musical dramaturgy in opera, not as a compositional technique per se. Since the text of the *Requiem* lacked dialogue occurring in real time, he felt no need to exploit the technique of *parlante*.

In most operas there is a one-to-one mapping between each singer and the character he or she portrays, in that throughout the opera the utterances of a singer can always be ascribed to the same character (whether the *character* is thinking, speaking, or, in the case of stage music, actually singing). The case of the *Requiem* is more complex: singers may step in and out of character. In the 'Confutatis maledictis' the bass represents alternately a narrator and cowed sinner. And while soprano and mezzo-soprano have moments in which they play the role of a terrified supplicant who can barely stammer out her words, in others (e.g., the 'Kyrie' or *Agnus Dei*) there is no reason to conceive of them as characters or even as a narrator.

It is intriguing that the most striking examples of the 'stammering topos', in the 'Liber scriptus' and the *Libera me,* belong to female soloists, although they hardly have a monopoly on its use. In both examples the women lose control of the musical discourse, unable to complete their thoughts, in a way that may bring to mind operatic depictions of madness or extreme anguish – and perhaps female madness and anguish in particular. Especially in the mezzo-soprano's final presentation of the line 'Nil inultum remanebit' of the 'Liber scriptus', the aimlessness of the vocal line is seconded by the aimless modulating sequence in the orchestra. (Compare the final bars of the bass's 'Mors stupebit', with its clearly directed descent from tonic to dominant.) And the most extreme example of lack of tonal control in the *Requiem* – at the opening of the *Lux æterna* – also features the mezzo-soprano. Furthermore, while Verdi assigned grovelling texts to the men as well – the 'Ingemisco' and the 'Confutatis maledictis' (with its second stanza 'Oro supplex et acclinis') – his setting belies the text: unlike the 'Liber scriptus' and *Libera me,* the men maintain control of their music, singing clearly shaped musical lines.

In any event, the fact that singers rapidly assume and just as rapidly discard their roles as characters means that consistency of characterization is not an issue in the *Requiem*: it is easier to identify the musical character of Azucena, Preziosilla, or Eboli than that of the mezzo-soprano in the *Requiem*. That is, there is no necessity that the part of each singer be either consistent in character throughout the work or differentiated in character from the other singers. The latter point is especially clear in the ensembles in the *Requiem*, which lack the dramatic conflict among participants that so often motivates Verdi's operatic ensembles, and in the *Requiem* ensembles all participants even sing the same text. In most of them, Verdi concentrates on developing his principal theme. (See the discussion of the 'Kyrie', 'Rex tremendæ', 'Lacrymosa', and *Offertorio*.) Moreover, once all the characters in an operatic 'conflict ensemble' have entered and they begin to sing together, the counterpoint is generally *non-imitative* (i.e., based upon the superimposition of different, contrasting, melodic lines) – the quartet in *Rigoletto* is a *locus classicus* – while *imitative* counterpoint prevails in the *Requiem*, and not merely in the fugues. Arnold Whittall writes, 'That the music of the *Requiem* is not just dramatic but operatic is confirmed by the use of a discarded duet from *Don Carlos* as the basis for the "Lacrimosa".'[15] But that the theme is all that Verdi could use of the duet shows how unoperatic the 'Lacrymosa' actually is. The duet involves conflict and incomprehension, and accordingly Carlos enters with material sharply contrasting with the lachrymose theme his father has just sung. Such considerations are not relevant in an ensemble like the 'Lacrymosa', and the bass may quite properly enter with the theme just presented by the mezzo-soprano, as she continues with a counterpoint to it.

The differences between the *Requiem* and Verdi's operas go beyond those attributable to the lack of a plot and the complex nature of the treatment of voice, however. The liturgically determined repetitions of text may generate (or at least suggest) large-scale musical structures not typical of the operas, for example the ABA of the 'Requiem æternam' (Introit), the return of the 'Quam olim Abrahæ' in the *Offertorio*, the repeated prayers in the *Agnus Dei*, realized here as a structure more closely resembling an instrumental theme and variations than anything in the operas. Time and time again Verdi beseeched his librettists for poetry with unusual structures. The text of the *Requiem* provided him with an opportunity and a challenge: all the texts are in prose except for the *Dies iræ*, which differs significantly from operatic verse (see p. 24). Although Verdi sometimes evokes, but only once adopts unmodified, the 'lyric prototype' so familiar from his operas, other passages are not even commensurable with it, as they consist of short phrases that are repeated and developed (e.g. the 'Kyrie', the principal section of the *Offertorio*, both fugues).

Furthermore, the *Requiem* shows no trace of the operatic cabaletta or even of the fast coda sometimes substituted for a full cabaletta (as in Lady Macbeth's 'La luce langue'). The dynamic of the slow movement followed by a faster movement serving as emotional vent, so basic to operatic structure, is entirely absent. What is more, in the *Requiem* – and in Verdi's sacred music in general – the range of tempos is narrower than in the operas. Tovey referred to Verdi's 'fundamental tempo for Church music: common time with [quarter-notes] ranging between 72 and 88 to the minute'.[16] The *Requiem* is indeed almost exclusively in common time ($\mathbf{C}$), with the exception of two examples each of rapid $\mathbf{\Phi}$ (the *Sanctus* and *Libera me* fugues, the fastest pieces in the *Requiem*) and of slow to moderate $\frac{6}{8}$ ('Quid sum miser' and the outer sections of the *Offertorio*).[17] As for the tempo of the pieces in $\frac{4}{4}$, if Tovey's 'fundamental tempo' were slightly extended to 66–96, only one piece would be slower ('Lacrymosa') and only three faster (the 'Quam olim Abrahæ' of the *Offertorio*, the introduction to the *Sanctus*, and the 'Dies iræ' music and its reprises). There are, then, few fast pieces in the *Requiem*, and except for the 'Quam olim Abrahæ', all are choruses. This contrasts with the operas: in *Aida*, for example, a few pieces (including 'O terra addio') are slower than Tovey's fundamental tempo, but many – predominantly pieces for the soloists – are faster. The *Requiem*, then, does eschew some of the variety of metres and rapid tempos found in the operas.

The 'Church music' topos in the *Requiem*

Since 'Church music' is a principal topos in nineteenth-century opera, it would be naive to claim that passages that evoke this idiom exorcize the spirit of opera and thus canonize the work as 'good Church music' (to use Crowest's phrase). But the situation is further complicated by the sharp disjunction between the tradition of sacred music actually intended to be sung in church and the operatic representation of 'church music', one subgenre of *couleur locale*. For example, the 'religious ceremony style' used by Verdi in *Il trovatore* or *La forza del destino* is seldom to be found in the *Requiem*. The second-act finale of *Forza*, with its organ prelude (note the 'churchy' decorated suspensions on the repetition of the opening phrase), and later, its prominent harp part, is as 'theatrical' – indeed, as 'operatic' – as anything Verdi ever wrote, but, ironically, had he written the entire *Requiem* in the saccharine devotional style of the 'La Vergine degli Angeli' perhaps no one might ever have criticized the work for being 'theatrical' or 'operatic'. In any event, organ and harp are used more in this operatic finale than in the entire corpus of Verdi's mature religious music, in which the organ appears not at all, and the harp for a mere dozen bars in the *Stabat Mater*. In this respect, and in others as well, Verdi's actual sacred music is decidedly at odds with both his *representation* of sacred music in his operas and some of the accepted, emblematic features of sacred music in general.

At least from Monteverdi's *Vespers* of 1610 and his enunciation, a few years earlier, of the dichotomy between first and second practice, church music has allowed a historicist menagerie of styles. Surely one such emblem of liturgical music would be references to plainchant or *falsobordone*. While I find no clear citations of pre-existent chant,[18] there are a few references to the general style. Let us consider the very opening of the *Libera me*, where the soloist declaims the text on a single tone in notes of roughly equal duration, 'senza misura'. In the context of a work of sacred music this naturally evokes plainchant, and this association obtains also at the openings of both Jago's 'Credo' and Desdemona's 'Ave Maria' in *Otello* – a mock prayer and a real prayer. However, in Verdi's operas, monotone declamation is more often used to represent proclamations than prayers; prayers are usually set as slow set-pieces.[19] There are, of course, other passages in the *Requiem* with declamation upon repeated notes, but all have features that block an association with psalmody: all are in strict tempo and many belong either to the 'supernatural declamatory style' (with exaggerated distinction between long and short durations) or the 'stammering topos'; somewhat later in the *Libera me* there is a monotone declamation within one of the few examples of *parlante* in the *Requiem*.

A few bars after the soprano's declamation at the opening of the *Libera me*, the chorus repeats the declamation upon a triad, adopting the technique of *falsobordone*. Here too the 'senza misura' delivery clearly associates the passage with liturgical practice, although this is hardly, if ever, found in Verdi's operatic representation of religious ceremonies. The usual religious chorus in opera – the 'Miserere' in *Il trovatore* is a good example – is very different; it is usually *a cappella* or doubled by the organ and, while often declamatory, perhaps with dotted rhythms, it will be organized in clear and symmetrical phrases. Nor does the *Requiem* make extensive use of the other musical style consecrated as appropriate for the church: the *stile antico*, i.e., what Verdi would have defined as the style of Palestrina. At most three passages invite comparison with the *stile antico*: the 'Te decet hymnus' (the Psalm verse of the 'Requiem æternam'), the opening of 'Quam olim Abrahæ' (*Offertorio*), and a passage in the *Lux æterna* (bb. 84–93). These are sung without accompaniment, or, in the 'Quam olim Abrahæ', lightly doubled by winds. In addition to this important sign of *stile antico*, all three passages begin with points of imitation which, once the stylistic point has been made, are quickly abandoned.[20] For extended uses of the *stile antico*, one must turn to the *Pater noster* of 1880 and the *Laudi alla Vergine Maria* (from the *Quattro pezzi sacri*). In the operas, however, this idiom is rarely found: an isolated instance is the sixteen-bar passage sung by the Priests near the beginning of the Act II Finale in *Aida*.[21]

Even though Verdi uses the idioms of plainchant and *stile antico* sparingly in his operas, they, like the chorale in *Die Meistersinger* or the ubiquitous organ in Verdi's church scenes, are unequivocal signs of the performance of music in church. On the other hand, the fugues in the *Requiem* fall squarely within the tradition of actual church music, not with the representation of church music in the theatre. Paradoxically, it would be inconceivable to depict, in an opera, the performance of music in a church through a fugue. The few fugues in Verdi's operas lack any religious connotation (e.g., the music of the conspirators in *Un ballo in maschera*, the battle in the 1865 version of *Macbeth*, the final 'burla' in *Falstaff*).

Other emblems of 'church music' are also eschewed. Neither in his operas nor in the *Requiem* does Verdi make significant use of concluding plagal cadences (despite a prominent instance at the end of the 'Requiem æternam' section of the *Libera me*). In his description of the *Pater noster* (see above) he defined Palestrina in terms of texture, regarding the harmony as an incidental feature of the style, and so it is not surprising that he does not follow Beethoven's example in adopting the church modes, even in his operatic representations of church music. Hardly any passages in the *Requiem* have a significant modal orientation (the harmonization of the principal melody of the 'Hostias' is as close as he comes). On the other hand, one might view the mysterious chromatic chords of the *Lux æterna*, especially when played tremolo in the high strings, as an operatic representation of the sacred that for Verdi goes back at least to Giselda's 'Salve Maria' in *I Lombardi*. Finally, the *Requiem* lacks liturgical-sounding cadences, with decorated suspensions or chains of suspensions (as when Don Carlo, disguised as a student, blesses the meal in *La forza del destino*, Act II scene i; the organ prelude at the beginning of the Act II Finale of the same work; or the 'Amen' of Bardolfo and Pistola in *Falstaff*, Act I).

Is the *Requiem* 'operatic,' then? Verdi did not forge a completely new style for it, and, since he is known primarily for his operas, it is understandable that unwary listeners might perceive another vocal work sharing some of the same local characteristics as 'operatic'. The sound is similar. And of course there are soloists, there is a bass drum, and there are exciting moments in both. But in important ways the *Requiem* is fundamentally different from Verdi's operas.

Notes

Preface

1 The most extensive survey of the work occupies thirty pages in Julian Budden's *Verdi*.
2 *The Works of Giuseppe Verdi* (Chicago and Milan, 1990), ser. 3, vol. I. Virtually all other editions in print are based upon a miniature score published by Ricordi in 1913, a score that drew the vocal parts from the printed piano-vocal reduction and the orchestral parts from an early Ricordi lithographed score.
3 The first-edition piano-vocal score of the 'Liber scriptus' is reproduced in my 'Verdi's "Liber scriptus" Rewritten'.
4 [Facsimile edition of Verdi's *Messa da Requiem*] (Milan, 1941); *Giuseppe Verdi, Libera me Domine – Messa per Rossini: Facsimile dell'autografo*, with a preface by Francesco Cossiga and an introduction by Pierluigi Petrobelli (Parma, 1988).
5 Directed by Helmuth Rilling, on Hänssler Classic 98.949.
6 On Verdi's rubato, see p. 17.

1 The genesis of the *Messa da Requiem per l'anniversario della morte di Manzoni 22 maggio 1874*

1 Verdi himself referred to the work in various ways, including 'Messa', 'Requiem', 'Messa da Requiem', 'Messa-Manzoni', and 'Messa da morto', but the official title he wanted to be used in publications is that given above. George Martin's perceptive article 'Verdi, Manzoni, and the *Requiem*' argues for the importance of the original title and the connection with Manzoni that it proclaims.
2 10 August 1868 letter to Giuseppe Piroli, in Luzio, *Carteggi verdiani*, vol. III, p. 56.
3 For this and the other references in this paragraph see Walker, *The Man Verdi*, pp. 345–6; Phillips-Matz, *Verdi*, pp. 544–7; Verdi's 27 August 1868 letter to Arrivabene (*Verdi intimo: Carteggio di Giuseppe Verdi con il conte Opprandino Arrivabene (1861–1886)*, ed. Annibale Alberti (Verona, 1931), pp. 96–7); and his 30 May 1868 letter to Piroli (Luzio, *Carteggi verdiani*, vol. III, pp. 53–4). Verdi was peeved about Rossini's response to Broglio's letter (see Phillips-Matz, *Verdi*, pp. 544–7).
4 It is ironic that Rossini had unsuccessfully attempted to persuade Pius IX to remove the ban on female singers in church.
5 Denis Mack Smith, *Italy: A Modern History* (Ann Arbor, 1959), rev. edn. (1969), p. 91.
6 For example, the Requiem of one Gherardo Gherardeschi performed in Pistoia, one composed by the professors of the Bologna Conservatory, one concocted from various numbers from Rossini's operas and from his *Stabat Mater*. See the discussion of 'Celebrazioni' in Carlo Matteo Mossa, 'Una "Messa" per la storia', in Girardi and Petrobelli, *Messa per Rossini*, pp. 17–25. The story of the *Messa per Rossini* is told more fully in Mossa's article and in the Introduction of *WGV*.
7 The committee was composed of Lauro Rossi, Alberto Mazzucato, and Stefano Ronchetti-

Monteviti, all of the Milan Conservatory, with Giulio Ricordi serving as secretary. From this point on, most of the correspondence cited here is not with Tito but Giulio Ricordi, who will be identified simply as 'Ricordi'.

8 According to an article presumably originating with the committee, the search was limited to successful operatic composers and composers with positions at the most renowned churches. Besides Verdi, the committee selected Antonio Bazzini, Raimondo Boucheron, Antonio Buzzola, Antonio Cagnoni, Carlo Coccia, Gaetano Gaspari, Teodulo Mabellini, Alessandro Nini, Carlo Pedrotti, Errico Petrella (who would later withdraw and be replaced by Lauro Rossi of the committee), Pietro Platania, and Federico Ricci. All but Bazzini, primarily a composer of instrumental music, met the stated criteria. Mercadante had refused on grounds of ill health. Verdi's copy of the prospectus has survived and is discussed in Marcus Engelhardt's 'Un opuscoletto di poche pagine', in Girardi and Petrobelli, *Messa per Rossini*, pp. 79–89; and in *WGV*. Most of the pages of the prospectus are reproduced in facsimile in Girardi and Petrobelli, *Messa per Rossini*.

9 Gatti, *Verdi* (1931), vol. II, p. 266, (1953) pp. 604 and 614, (1955) pp. 256 and 259; Luzio, *Carteggi verdiani*, vol. IV, p. 175.

10 Letter to Ricordi, drafted 27 December 1869, *WGV*, p. xv.

11 Note too that when Verdi proposed to write a Requiem Mass to be performed on the first anniversary of Manzoni's death he was still uncertain whether there would be four or five soloists (see the letter of 3 June 1874, written to Ricordi, cited below). It is hard to believe that the Mass was nearly completed if he still had not made such a fundamental decision as that.

12 And in 1858 he set some verses from *Adelchi* as an albumleaf for a Neapolitan friend. See Phillips-Matz, *Verdi*, p. 377.

13 Letter to Clara Maffei, early July 1868, in Abbiati, *Giuseppe Verdi*, vol. III, p. 215, translation after William Weaver, *Verdi: A Documentary Study*, p. 220.

14 The diagnosis of the attending doctors Gherini and Todeschini was initially given as acute cerebral meningitis, then corrected to chronic cerebral meningitis.

15 James Hepokoski, 'Verdi's "Requiem": A Memorial for an Epoch', in liner notes for Deutsche Grammophon Compact Disc 423 674-2 (recording of the *Requiem* with Carlo Maria Giulini and the Berlin Philharmonic Orchestra); Rubens Tedeschi, 'Requiem per il Risorgimento', program book for Teatro alla Scala, 14 September 1985 performance of Verdi's *Requiem*, pp. 5–9.

16 After preliminary sketching, Verdi entered vocal parts (including text), bass line, and some of the other important instrumental lines into the appropriate staves of his emerging autograph score, returning later to complete the orchestration. This initial layer is the so-called *skeleton score*. Of course many composers worked this way (with or without the preliminary sketching); indeed, the term 'skeleton score' goes at least as far back as Tovey's note on the overture to *Die Zauberflöte*.

17 The chords in Berlioz's 'Hostias', with three closely spaced flutes in the upper register and trombones below, are echoed in the opening scene with the Monk and off-stage chorus in Act II (of the five-act versions) of *Don Carlos*. Verdi's and Berlioz's settings of the 'Tuba mirum' are compared below (pp. 26–7).

18 Another aspect of Verdi's preparation was to copy out the text of the *Dies iræ* and the *Offertorio* and to sketch a prose translation; he also took notes about Latin declamation and syllabic division in his copy of the *Messa per Rossini* prospectus. (Beethoven had taken similar steps in readying himself for the composition of the *Missa Solemnis*; see William Drabkin, *Beethoven: 'Missa solemnis'* [Cambridge, 1991], p. 14.)

19 However, Verdi subdivided some of the seven sections of its *Dies iræ*, with the result that his movement has ten sections, considerably more than in the *Dies iræ* settings of Mozart, Cherubini, or Berlioz.

20 One should not exaggerate the significance of the few similarities in the choice of performing

group – the 'Ingemisco' for tenor solo, the 'Confutatis' for bass (in a sharp key), *Lux æterna* for three soloists (to be performed at a moderate tempo).

21 The adoption of four bassoons and ophicleide reflects French practice, as Marcello Conati has noted ('L'orchestra della "Messa" per Rossini: appunti e considerazioni in margine', in Girardi and Petrobelli, *Messa per Rossini*, p. 115).

22 See Hussey, *Verdi*, pp. 200–8, for the mistaken revisionist view that in 1874 Verdi scrapped all but the opening section and fugue of the 1869 *Libera me*.

2 **The premiere, subsequent performance history, and performing practices**

1 *La nuova illustrazione universale*, 14 June 1874.

2 The *Gazzetta*, which opposed municipal funding for the *Requiem*, had raised doubts about Manzoni's legacy immediately after the writer's death – asking whether his principles had been beneficial to Italy or had served instead to slow its progress (cited in *Il pungolo*, 24 May 1873).

3 The contract with Ricordi specifies that the composer was to receive 50 per cent of the rental fees paid to the publisher. The contract with Escudier, who had complete rights only for France and Belgium and the right to compete with Ricordi in England, does not specify the amount of royalties to be paid (except for England, again 50 per cent). At least in France, Verdi would receive the usual *droits d'auteur*.

4 The 8182.09 lire received by the city covered about 80 per cent of its expenses for the Manzoni commemoration in San Marco.

5 For purposes of comparison: Stolz (soprano) and Waldmann (mezzo-soprano) each earned 3,000 lire; Capponi (tenor), 2,600; Maini (bass), 1,800; Faccio, only 500; the chorus master, 300; the custodian, a mere 40 lire.

6 'Musikalisches aus Italien', p. 341. The report, primarily concerned with the failure of Glinka's *A Life for the Tsar* at Milan's Teatro dal Verme, is a broad attack on Italian culture (musical and otherwise), and it did not fail to stir up the Italian press.

7 Ricordi's preferred practice was to rent performance material rather than sell it outright.

8 For a summary of the reviews, see Toye, *Giuseppe Verdi*, pp. 149–51.

9 Monaldi writes that the decline in the number of performances started as early as 1875 and suggests that it was partly due to the retirement of Waldmann and Stolz. See Monaldi, *Verdi*, p. 264.

10 Kate Hevner Mueller, *Twenty-Seven Major American Symphony Orchestras: A History and Analysis of their Repertoires – Seasons 1842–43 through 1969–70* (Bloomington, Indiana, 1973), pp. 363–4.

11 'Stolz [Stolzová], Teresa' (by Andrew Porter), in *The New Grove Dictionary of Music and Musicians*, ed. S. Sadie, 20 vols. (London, 1980). The contemporary account, quoted by Porter, comes from Blanche Roosevelt's report on the 1875 Paris performances for the *Chicago Times*, reprinted in her *Verdi: Milan and 'Othello'* (London, 1887), pp. 73–4.

12 According to Blanche Roosevelt, 'Waldmann's organ is so much like a tenor's that you can hardly realize that a woman is singing', *Verdi: Milan and 'Othello'*, p. 73. The range of the mezzo-soprano part in the *Requiem* (g to g^2, with a single ab^2, added in the 1875 'Liber scriptus') is precisely that of Ulrica in *Un ballo in maschera*.

13 See Jon W. Finson, 'Performing Practice in the Late Nineteenth Century, with Special Reference to the Music of Brahms', *Musical Quarterly* 62 (1984), pp. 468–71; Clive Brown, 'Bowing Styles, Vibrato and Portamento in Nineteenth-Century Violin Playing', *Journal of the Royal Musical Association* 113 (1988), pp. 97–128.

14 They normally would have transposed unplayable notes an octave higher. To prevent this in an exposed passage in the 'Quid sum miser', Verdi specifies that those players without the low G should simply omit the note.

15 While a tenor tuba (or euphonium) might best imitate the sound of an ophicleide, Verdi

probably would have preferred the homogeneity of sound provided by a bass trombone. See *WGV*, p. xxxiv, and Renato Meucci, 'Il cimbasso e gli strumenti affini nell'Ottocento italiano', *Studi verdiani* 5 (1989), pp. 109–62.

16 From the *Kölnische Zeitung* (22 May 1877, no. 141): Marcello Conati, ed., *Encounters with Verdi*, tr. Richard Stokes (Ithaca, 1984), pp. 125–7.

17 For both the *Stabat Mater* and *Te Deum* Verdi specified, 'The whole of this piece should be performed at the same tempo, indicated by the metronome mark. Nonetheless, at certain points it is appropriate to slow down or speed up for the sake of expressiveness and colouring, always returning to the *Primo tempo*, however.'

3 *Requiem e Kyrie*

1 The relationship of the two passages is discussed below, pp. 67–8.
2 Hanslick, 'Verdi's Requiem' (Pleasants translation), p. 165.
3 Verdi's setting recalls the 'Te decet hymnus' of Cherubini's C-minor Requiem (although there the orchestra discreetly doubles the vocal parts).
4 Budden, *Verdi*, p. 321.
5 Tovey, 'Requiem', p. 200.
6 The relationship to the principal theme is even clearer in an earlier, erased layer in the autograph in which the rhythm of the first bar was identical to that of Ex. 3.1b.

4 *Dies iræ*

1 'Dies iræ' (Section 1, by John Caldwell), in *The New Grove*.
2 In the reprises Verdi writes out the choral parts, usually the cello and contrabass parts, and in the first reprise only, the first violin part as well.
3 In this calculation, I do not count an *immediate* repetition of text, like the repetition of the Verse in the *Lux æterna*, as an extra-liturgical reprise.
4 This is not typical of Verdi's *œuvre* as a whole, however: in his operas, and in the *Stabat mater* and *Te Deum*, musical reprises freely occur with new text.
5 Budden, *Verdi*, p. 322.
6 Here too I am indebted to Budden's account. For ritual scenes (discussed below) and the use of the anapestic motive to signify death, see chapters 8 and 10 of Frits Noske's *The Signifier and the Signified: Studies in the Operas of Mozart and Verdi* (The Hague, 1977). But as a necessary corrective, see also Winton Dean's review in *19th Century Music* 2 (1978–9), pp. 173–8.
7 Reyer, 'Requiem de Verdi', pp. 362–5. Neither Cherubini, Berlioz, nor Verdi felt obliged to limit themselves to a single brass instrument in evoking 'tuba mirum', as Mozart had done. Apparently a literal-minded critic found fault with Verdi's procedure (see Monaldi, *Verdi*, pp. 258–9).
8 Verdi's letter to Maria Waldmann of 5 March 1875 in Luzio, *Carteggi verdiani*, vol. II, pp. 239–40.
9 The reasons for Verdi's decision to replace the original version are discussed in Chapter 10.
10 The subscripts indicate the number of bars. See Joseph Kerman, '"Lyric Form" and Flexibility in "Simon Boccanegra"', *Studi verdiani* 1 (1982), pp. 47–62. Note that the 'lyric prototype' (Kerman's term) may describe either an aria or one singer's presentation of a double quatrain within a larger form, and that this scheme covers only the initial presentation of the text. After this point, especially in solo numbers, a coda will generally follow, based upon the repetition of text already stated. By the late 1850s, 'A new lyric prototype can be discerned, $[a_4 \; a'_4 \; c_4]$ in addition to $[a_4 \; a'_4 \; b_4 \; c_4]$' (*ibid.*, p. 58).
11 Curiously, the repeated a's stem from the fourth bar of the fugue subject of the original setting, on the text 'totum conti[netur]'. Pierluigi Petrobelli has noted that, in revising, Verdi often preserves some element of the original version, rather than starting from scratch ('Osservazioni

sul processo compositivo in Verdi', *Acta musicologica* 43 (1971), pp. 125–42). Another example is Verdi's revision of the opening of the 'Dies iræ' music (see pp. 64–7 below).

12 See Ex. 11.1c and 11.1e, *Dies iræ*, bb. 604–8 (the choral sopranos), *Libera me*, bb. 392–400.

13 Marco Beghelli has applied the philosopher J. L. Austin's distinction between 'performative' and 'constative' speech acts to Verdi's musical dramaturgy. See his 'Atti performativi nella drammaturgia verdiana' (Dissertation, University of Bologna [tesi di laurea] 1986) and, more accessible, 'Per un nuovo approccio'.

14 The chorus intoned these words at bars 177, 191, and 213 as well, but only at the end of the solo does it begin to insist upon them, repeating them every two bars (bars 229, 231, 233). Verdi had entered into the autograph score additional choral interjections at bars 206, 208, and 210 as well, but later cancelled them, probably to avoid anticipating – and thus weakening – the effect at the end of the solo.

15 Beghelli discusses the lamento topos in 'Atti performativi', pp. 45–81; and in 'Per un nuovo approccio', pp. 634–7.

16 Ursula Kirkendale, 'The King of Heaven and the King of France: History of a Musical Topos', in *Abstracts of Papers Read at the Thirty-Fifth Annual Meeting of the American Musicological Society*, Saint Louis, Missouri, 27–9 December 1969, pp. 27–8.

17 This gesture echoes the opening of the 'Rex tremendæ' section, a violent answer to the questions fearfully posed at the end of the preceding section, the 'Quid sum miser'.

18 There is an example of this procedure in each of the three quartets with chorus: see *Requiem æternam e Kyrie*, bb. 97–101 and *Dies iræ*, bb. 657–65 (in the 'Lacrymosa').

19 James Hepokoski, 'Verdi's "Requiem": A Memorial for an Epoch', in liner notes for Deutsche Grammophon Compact Disc 423 674-2 (recording of the *Requiem* with Carlo Maria Giulini and the Berlin Philharmonic Orchestra).

20 [George] Bernard Shaw, 'A Word More about Verdi' (originally published in *The Anglo-Saxon Review* of March 1901), in *Shaw's Music: The Complete Musical Criticism in Three Volumes*, ed. Dan H. Laurence, 3 vols. (New York 1981), vol. III, p. 582.

21 In the first movement of the 'Eroica' Symphony, for example, the opening theme is destabilized by the mysterious C♯, but, by the end of the movement, it has been stabilized in a new, militantly diatonic version that rocks back and forth from I to V^7 in symmetrical four-bar blocks. The procedure is also related to the so-called 'sonata principle', which 'requires that important statements made in a key other than the tonic must either be re-stated in the tonic, or brought into a closer relation with the tonic, before the movement ends'. Edward T. Cone, *Musical Form and Musical Performance* (New York, 1968), pp. 76–7. See also Charles Rosen, *The Classical Style: Haydn, Mozart, Beethoven* (New York, 1972), pp. 26, 72–4; and *Sonata Forms*, rev. edn. (New York, 1988), pp. 25–6.

22 This theme will reappear in the 1883 version of *Don Carlos*: see the final duet of Elisabeth and Don Carlos, beginning eighteen bars before the Marziale.

23 Filippi, Review of the premiere; Reyer, 'Requiem de Verdi', pp. 366–7; Hanslick, 'Verdi's Requiem', p. 165.

24 However, since this section lacks the contrast between chorus and solo seen in the 'Rex tremendæ', some readers may prefer Budden's formulation: 'the bass soloist stands for both priest and supplicant, so embracing the two poles of sternness and entreaty on which the movement rests'. Budden, *Verdi*, p. 328.

25 According to Reyer, the excuse for the fifths could no longer be found in their originality of effect, as with those of the 'choeur des cloches' of *Guillaume Tell* (see the following note for appropriate reference). At least for French and Italian writers, Rossini's passage (Act II, scene I, opening chorus, on the text 'Voici la nuit') was a *locus classicus*, a much more celebrated example of parallel triads than those at the beginning of the coda of the first movement of the 'Eroica' Symphony (which Berlioz, in his review of *Guillaume Tell*, cited in defence of Rossini's). Verdi termed them *'bellissime*, especially for the colour' – comparing them favourably even to a passage in a 'Stabat mater' of his beloved Palestrina; letter of 15 June 1893

to Cesare de Sanctis (author of a harmony treatise), in Emilia Zanetti, 'La corrispondenza di Verdi conservata a "S. Cecilia": Contributi all'epistolario', in *Verdi: Bollettino dell'Istituto di studi verdiani*, vol. III, no. 8, p. 1137; and, in English and German translation, pp. 1495–6.

26 References for this paragraph: Hanslick, 'Verdi's Requiem', pp. 165–6; Reyer, 'Requiem de Verdi', p. 361; Felix Salzer, *Structural Hearing: Tonal Coherence in Music*, 2 vols. (New York, 1962), vol. I, p. 198; vol. II, p. 192 (ex. 429); Tovey, 'Requiem', p. 203; Budden, *Verdi*, pp. 328–9.

27 Reyer, 'Requiem de Verdi', p. 367.

28 Reyer, 'Requiem de Verdi', pp. 361 and 369; Filippi, Review of the first La Scala performance.

29 Reyer, 'Requiem de Verdi', p. 367.

30 Filippi, Review of the first La Scala performance. While the music may evoke 'Religious Music', the passage it most closely resembles is a moment of terrible irony in *Don Carlos*, where the Grand Inquisitor tells Philippe, 'Rentrez dans le devoir! L'Eglise, en bonne mère, / peut encore accueillir un repentir sincère', and then asks him to deliver up Posa.

5 *Offertorio*

1 Budden, *Verdi*, p. 330; Hussey, *Verdi*, p. 224.

2 The section ends with another recollection of 'Lassù in ciel', where divided violins have pizzicato downbeats with arco offbeats.

3 Unlike the similar setting of the 'Te decet hymnus' (the Psalm of the 'Requiem æternam'), the treatment here suggests a canon, as the motive invariably appears at the same pitch class, rather than with the alternation of tonic and dominant characteristic of fugue.

4 Hussey, *Verdi*, p. 224; Robertson, *Music of Mourning*, p. 107.

5 Filippo Filippi, Review of the premiere and Review of the first La Scala performance.

6 Salvatore Farina, in the 31 May 1874 issue of *Gazzetta musicale di Milano*.

7 At the beginning of this reprise the voices are marked *forte* rather than *piano*. The orchestra will surely need to increase its dynamic level as well.

8 The reprise of text from the verse – 'Fac eas de morte transire ad vitam' – is not accompanied by a reprise of the music originally associated with it, but with that of the opening section. This line is the only one in the *Offertorio* that makes such a direct, personal plea for a positive outcome (salvation). Since the musical resolution brings peace, this text makes a more appropriate close than would those lines with images of the lion's mouth and the bottomless pit.

9 An ominous chromatic inflection (B♮ alternating with C) may suggest the alternation of minor with major triads, but does not challenge the primacy of the tonic.

6 *Sanctus*

1 Adagio (Mozart), Andante (Cherubini's C-minor Requiem), Andante un poco sostenuto e maestoso (Berlioz), Maestoso (Cherubini's D-minor Requiem and the *Messa per Rossini*). The fastest tempo of Verdi's potential models, though not in a Requiem, is the Andantino mosso of the *Sanctus* of Rossini's *Petite Messe solennelle*.

2 The prospectus for the *Messa per Rossini* prescribed a single tempo for the entire movement, but in the event, Platania provided a fast fugue for the 'Hosanna'. Cherubini, like Verdi, does not divide the text into different sections.

3 Most of the generalizations in this paragraph also apply to the fugal treatment of the 'Liber scriptus', replaced in 1875 by the mezzo-soprano solo.

4 To follow the normal procedure used in analysing Bach fugues would force us to set aside common sense and analyse the *Sanctus* as a fugal exposition plus an enormous episode in which the subject (i.e., the complete subject) never appears, but in which references to it are virtually never absent.

5 In the performances Verdi directed, he generally placed the chorus in a column on the spectators' right, with the orchestra on their left – an arrangement that would have diluted the antiphonal and polychoral effects in (especially) the exposition and final section of the *Sanctus* fugue.

6 The 'lyric prototype' is discussed on pp. 28–9 above. Because of the long note-values, the structure unfolds in 32 bars rather than the usual 16.

7 *Agnus Dei*

1 This formulation emphasizes the movement's resemblance to the Theme and Variations, a standard form of instrumental music – especially German instrumental music – and therefore privileges the element of change unfolding in the orchestral accompaniment. Most contemporary critics placed their emphasis differently, however. Privileging the vocal parts, they described the procedure as repetition (of a vocal phrase). The element of variation in the orchestral accompaniment was regarded as secondary and, in some reviews, not noted at all.

2 Blanche Roosevelt, *Verdi: Milan and 'Othello'*, p. 73.

3 Some resemblances to opera have also been noted, however. Filippi, Review of the premiere, was reminded of 'the famous sixteen bars of Meyerbeer's *L'Africaine*' (probably the passage at the beginning of Selica's scene near the end, 'D'ici je vois la mer'), and Budden remarks that the cadence figure 'has been encountered as early as Giselda's death scene in *I Lombardi*', Budden, *Verdi*, p. 332.

4 Tovey, 'Requiem', p. 206.

5 The manoeuvre may recall moments like bars 29–33 of Beethoven's Piano Sonata in D, Op. 10 No. 3, IV, where a passage that originally led to a V–vi deceptive cadence is repeated, leading not to the expected authentic cadence (V–I), but to another, more intense, deceptive cadence: V–♭VI.

8 *Lux æterna*

1 The connection between the two passages was noted by Ernest Reyer (in 'Requiem de Verdi'). The first appearance of Meyerbeer's passage can be found in *The New Oxford History of Music*, vol. IX (*Romanticism (1830–90)*), ed. Gerald Abraham (Oxford and New York, 1990), p. 118. For Verdi's admiration of the scene, see Abbiati, *Giuseppe Verdi*, vol. II, p. 794.

2 Central to John Roeder's interpretation of the *Lux æterna* is his (to my mind) dubious linking of this fleeting G-minor chord with the opening of the *Dies iræ* movement and the idea of the day of wrath – see his 'Pitch and Rhythmic Dramaturgy'. I consider some aspects of the article in my 'Reprise as Resolution'.

3 *Il Secolo*, excerpt reprinted in the 24 May 1874 issue of *Gazzetta musicale di Milano*.

4 The recurrence at bb. 100–3 of the flute and clarinet figure refers back to section D' ('Cum Sanctis tuis . . .'); however, since that section was presented in the tonic major at the outset, it would be difficult to argue that the recurrence is needed to provide resolution.

9 The *Libera me* and its genesis

1 For more thorough treatments of the revision, see my '*Messa* a Rossini' (Part 2) and 'Genesis', chapter 4, pp. 74–129. Two sources of the 1869 score are available, Appendix 2 of *WGV* and a facsimile of Verdi's autograph manuscript (see Preface, note 4, for references).

2 By contrast the 1869 version is rhythmically square and harmonically unadventurous (1869: 15–19).

3 The term is from Abramo Basevi's *Studio sulle opere di Verdi* (Florence, 1859), pp. 30–1.

4 The broken arpeggio figuration in the strings will reappear in the new Act I finale of *Simon Boccanegra*, composed in 1880–1.

5 The alternation of V⁷/V and V⁷ foreshadows the similar procedure in the 'Dies iræ' section (bb. 90–105), but in the later passage there is no resolution.

6 Leonard Meyer, *Emotion and Meaning in Music* (Chicago 1956), p. 171.

7 Stolz's vocal characteristics are discussed above, p. 15.

8 In both versions of the movement Verdi inverts the 'Dies illa, dies iræ' of the liturgical text, making it correspond to the opening of the *Dies iræ*. Of course there can have been no question of a musical reprise in the collaborative *Messa per Rossini*.

9 Ending the previous section on a C-*major* chord heightens the disjunctive and disruptive effect; compare the 1869 version.

10 The autograph of the *Dies iræ* movement shows that Verdi originally had conceived of the scale passage in the ninth and tenth bars of this passage as a single bar. He expanded it to two bars – thus eliminating the awkward effect of two successive metrically strong bars – after copying the vocal parts into the second reprise of the passage but before preparing the autograph of the *Libera me*.

11 In both versions, but especially the first, this moment recalls the transition to the largo concertato concluding Act II of *Macbeth*.

12 It is not known whether Verdi, when he wrote the opening 'Requiem æternam' in A minor, had already decided to transpose the reprise to B♭, or whether he had at the time expected that both appearances of this music would be in A, deciding upon the transposition only later.

13 A few examples are cited in my 'Genesis', p. 185.

14 Filippi, Review of the first La Scala performance, wrote that the reprise was a semitone higher 'for greater effect', probably referring to the greater intensity afforded by the higher pitch; Joseph Braunstein, pointing to Verdi's predilection for flat keys for death scenes, thought the 'choice of a flat key for the final part of the *Requiem* was a foregone conclusion' ('Celestial Salute', *Opera News*, 19 March 1951, p. 32). (Both Filippi and Braunstein were unaware that the passage had been in A minor in the 1869 movement.) John Roeder emphasizes the importance of 'the sudden integration' of the thematic material of the opening 'Requiem æternam' with the key of 'dramatically crucial elements of large sections of the mass', namely, the two other areas in B♭ minor-major, the 'Lacrymosa' and the *Lux æterna* ('Pitch and Rhythmic Dramaturgy', p. 185). One might point to, to use David Lawton's term, the 'double cycle' created by the transposition: the G-minor 'Dies iræ' music leads to B♭ minor at the end of the *Dies iræ* and again in the *Libera me*; moreover, C and B♭ alternate in the last three movements of the *Messa da Requiem*: *Agnus Dei* – C; *Lux æterna* – B♭; – *Libera me* – c – (g) – b♭/B♭ – c/C.

15 See James A. Hepokoski, 'Verdi's Composition of *Otello*: The Act II Quartet', in *Analyzing Opera: Verdi and Wagner*, ed. Carolyn Abbate and Roger Parker (Berkeley, 1989), pp. 125–49, especially at 143–9. For an example from *Don Carlos*, see Ursula Günther, 'La Genèse de *Don Carlos*, opéra en cinq actes de Giuseppe Verdi, représenté pour la première fois à Paris le 11 mars 1867', *Revue de Musicologie* 68 (1972), pp. 45–8 and 53–6.

16 In the 1869 version there was a similar effect: the strings had two bars of tremolo (on an open fifth A–E) before the soprano re-entered. The 1913 Ricordi miniature score, the source of almost all scores in print, erroneously inserted the soprano's fermata and rest into the string parts as well, so that the soloist and strings enter simultaneously.

17 The duration is difficult to determine because of the 'senza misura', 'poco allargando', and 'morendo' indications in the last six bars of the movement. Until then Verdi's metronome markings indicate 4'5"; Toscanini takes 4'52" for the entire fugue, while Muti's 1987 recording allots it 5'49", of which one minute (about 17 per cent of the total) is dedicated to the last six bars!

18 References for this paragraph: Tovey, 'Requiem', pp. 208–9; Toye, *Giuseppe Verdi*, pp. 390–2; Hanslick, 'Verdi's Requiem', pp. 163–4; Hussey, *Verdi*, pp. 208–9.

19 'Requiem', p. 208. Of course, the voice-leading of the vocal parts presupposes the support of the orchestral chords: note, for example, the inadmissible dissonant fourth that would have

occurred on the downbeat of b. 186 without them. In the 1869 version, incidentally, the cadences were marked even more strongly, as trumpets doubled the last four notes of the subject.

20 The original version of the passage included a dialogue between flute and bassoon in which the opening motive of the inverted subject is passed back and forth at its original pace. Verdi may have found it a distraction from the lyricism of this moment, but it remains a curious alteration: unlike most of his revisions, it results in a less complex texture rather than a denser one.

21 Symptomatic of this is her liberation from the onerous duty of doubling the choral sopranos: in the 1869 version she did so for more than a third of the section – 39 of the 110 bars – in the final version she does so for only eleven bars (including seven bars where her text is different, but the music otherwise identical).

22 This revision is similar in aim to that of two others: the penultimate bar of the 'Lacrymosa' theme (see pp. 78–9 below) and the soprano's descending line in *Libera me*, bb. 4–6.

23 See bb. 233–8 and 262–76 (the augmentation) from the fugue, as well as bb. 75–83 from the 'Dies iræ music'.

24 Roeder, 'Pitch and Rhythmic Dramaturgy', p. 185.

25 Budden, *Verdi*, p. 335. See also George Martin's refutation of the view that finds in Verdi's *Requiem* a 'trusting and childlike fearlessness before God' and the conception that death is not a terrible vision but a friend. Martin, 'Verdi, Manzoni, and the Requiem', p. 52. Incidentally, there is no indication in Verdi's score prescribing that the declamation should be sung more slowly here than in the other two presentations. In the 1869 version, however, Verdi notated the declamation of the basses in quarter-notes, rather than the eighth-notes of the opening.

26 References for this paragraph: Reyer, 'Requiem de Verdi', p. 369; Toye, *Giuseppe Verdi*, pp. 390 and 392.

27 See Verdi's 1 March 1896 letter to Giovanni Tebaldini about the *Te Deum*: 'it ends with a prayer ... *Dignare Domine die isto* ... moving, gloomy, sad to the point of terror'. See Abbiati, *Giuseppe Verdi*, vol. IV, pp. 588–9.

28 Notes to the Toscanini recording of the *Missa solemnis* (RCA LM 6013), cited by Maynard Solomon, *Beethoven* (New York, 1977), p. 309.

10   Two revisions

1 For a fuller treatment of these revisions, see my 'Verdi's "Liber scriptus" Rewritten', 'Operatic Origins', and 'Genesis', chapters 5–6. The relevant musical sources are cited in the Preface, and in note 3 below.

2 For example, Alberto Mazzucato, who praised the *Sanctus* and *Libera me* fugues, but found that the text of the 'Liber scriptus' would have been more appropriately expressed by 'melopee salmodiche o palestriniane' (*Gazzetta musicale di Milano*, 21 June 1874); Ernest Reyer, who described the fugue as 'un peu trop sautillante' ('Requiem de Verdi', p. 365); or the reviewer in the *Corriere di Milano* who found it 'too theatrical and, we would say, almost choreographic' (reprinted in the 24 May 1874 number of *Gazzetta musicale di Milano*).

3 Filippi came even closer than Tovey, associating 'the dramatic character of the melody' with *Don Carlos* (*Gazzetta musicale di Milano*, 28 May 1874). For the circumstances surrounding the cut, see my 'Operatic Origins', pp. 65–6, and other sources cited there. The duet is printed in piano-vocal score in *Giuseppe Verdi, 'Don Carlos'; Edizione integrale delle varie versioni* [. . .], ed. Ursula Günther and Luciano Petazzoni, 2 vols. (Milan, 1980), vol. II, pp. 553–63.

11   The *unità musicale* of the *Requiem*

1 Letter to Tito Ricordi, May 1868, in Abbiati, *Giuseppe Verdi*, vol. III, p. 200.

2 Letter to Cesare Vigna of 9 September 1854, concerning a proposed pasticcio about Joan of Arc, in Giannetto Bongiovanni, *Dal carteggio inedito Verdi-Vigna* (Rome, 1941), pp. 44–5. The question of *tinta* or *colorito* is also relevant here. For two recent discussions of this elusive concept, see Harold Powers, "'La solita forma" and "The Uses of Convention"', *Acta musicologica* 59 (1987), pp. 65–90; and Gilles de Van, 'La notion de "tinta": mémoire confuse et affinités thématiques dans les opéras de Verdi', *Revue de Musicologie* 76 (1990), pp. 187–98.

3 Of these only Paisiello's work concludes with the *Libera me* movement, and, as in Verdi's, both Introit and *Dies iræ* movements are recapitulated. It is unlikely that Verdi was familiar with the Haydn or Paisiello works.

4 In the 'Quantus tremor' passage of the 'Dies iræ', 'Mors stupebit', 'Liber scriptus', 'Ingemisco' (third stanza), and 'Lacrymosa'.

5 In the 1869 *Libera me* all sections but the fugue were linked through the tempo of ♩ = 72 or 144. In the 1874 version, the 'Liber scriptus' fugue was exactly twice the speed of the 'Mors stupebit' (♩ = 144 and 72, respectively).

6 There are also more distant sections performed at these tempos. In the 'Quid sum miser' the ♩. proceeds at almost half of 66; both the 'Te decet hymnus' section of the 'Requiem æternam' and the *Lux æterna* are paced at ♩ = 88. For Verdi's use of recurring metronome markings in his operas, see John Mauceri, '*Rigoletto* for the 21st Century', *Opera* 36 (1985), pp. 1135–44; Andrew Porter, 'Marking Time', *The New Yorker*, 30 May 1985, pp. 95–6; David Lawton, Introduction to the critical edition of *Il trovatore*, *Works of Giuseppe Verdi* (Chicago and Milan, 1993), ser. 1, vol. XVIIIA, p. xxxi.

7 Elsewhere I argue that Verdi probably chose the key of B♭ minor for the 'Lacrymosa' – it is the same key as the *Don Carlos* duet – primarily because the theme lies well for the bass voice in that key. Indeed, given the wide range of the theme (especially since the opening motive is later sung an octave lower), there are almost no other keys in which he could sing it. On the other hand, the part lies unexpectedly low for the mezzo-soprano, rising only to e♭^{2}. That she happens to begin the 'Lacrymosa' is of course immaterial. See Rosen, 'Genesis', pp. 135–7.

8 Only the 'Recordare' ends with the strong closure provided by an authentic cadence followed by a pause, but in compensation, the next section ('Ingemisco') opens by repeating, a step lower, the concluding motive of the 'Recordare'.

9 There is a third-relation between the *Offertorio* and the *Sanctus*; only the *Sanctus* and the *Agnus Dei* are related by a fifth.

10 On the role of organicist theories in music analysis and musicology see Ruth A. Solie, 'The Living Work: Organicism and Musical Analysis', *19th Century Music* 4 (1980), pp. 147–56; also Janet Levy, 'Covert and Casual Values in Recent Writings about Music', *Journal of Musicology* 5 (1987), pp. 3–27.

12 A question of genre

1 Drabkin, *Beethoven: 'Missa solemnis'*, pp. 19–20.

2 Frederick J. Crowest, *Verdi: Man and Musician: His Biography with Especial Reference to his English Experiences* (New York, 1897), repr. edn. (New York, 1978), pp. 158–60.

3 Toye, *Giuseppe Verdi*, pp. 437–8. To maintain this view, Toye needed to draw the corollary: 'It is surprising how readily the music lends itself to visual interpretation. In the opening bars we can imagine the chorus kneeling in whispered prayer for the repose of the soul; the *Kyrie* is a definite appeal for mercy.' This is unhelpful: the attempt to posit a latent staging for the entire work obfuscates the tension between those moments that do suggest such an interpretation (e.g., the opening of the *Libera me*) and those that do not (e.g., the 'Kyrie'). For a slightly more cautious claim for the representational nature of the *Requiem*, see Pizzetti, 'La religiosità di Verdi', pp. 211–13.

4　It was apparently performed in the cathedral of Barcelona 'for the funeral of Queen Mercedes' (*Gazzetta musicale di Milano*, 4 August 1877, p. 277), but performances in church were very rare. Monaldi claimed that the performance in the cathedral of Orvieto in 1892 was the first in a church since the work's premiere (Monaldi, *Verdi*, p. 264).

5　The remaining mature sacred works of Verdi were all premiered in a theatre or concert hall rather than in church.

6　Hanslick, 'Verdi's Requiem', p. 162.

7　This excerpt is from the December 1869 letter quoted on p. 4.

8　Hanslick, 'Verdi's Requiem', p. 161.

9　David G. Hughes, *A History of European Music: The Art Music Tradition of Western Culture* (New York, 1974), p. 429.

10　See pp. 8 and 17. Note also that he opposed publishing the piano–vocal score as separately purchasable 'pezzi staccati', the method used for his operas up to that time, wanting to avoid 'that odour of *arias*, duets, trios, quartets, etc. etc.'. And the titles and descriptions that he suggested for the table of contents avoid 'operatic' terms like 'quartetto' and 'aria', preferring 'a quattro parti' and 'Solo per Basso', and call attention to the use of fugue in the *Sanctus* and *Libera me*.

11　On the negative connotations of 'operatic', see Levy, 'Covert and Casual Values in Recent Writings', pp. 12–13.

12　Letter to Vigna, 12 June 1875. Abbiati, *Giuseppe Verdi*, vol. III, p. 753. See also Toye's comment, 'How could [the words of the Requiem Mass] be interpreted in any other way by a man like Verdi, to whom theatrical expression was second nature? . . . Any other kind of setting would have been a proof, not of deep sincerity, but of insincerity, at least of self-conscious pedantry on his part.' (Toye, *Giuseppe Verdi*, pp. 388–9.)

13　Letter to Hiller of 7 January 1880, in Luzio, *Carteggi verdiani*, vol. II, p. 333.

14　Hanslick, however, noted (in 'Verdi's Requiem', p. 165) that the *Requiem* and *Aida* 'are about as self-sufficient and individual in relation to one another as any two works by the same composer could very well be'.

15　Arnold Whittall, *Romantic Music: A Concise History from Schubert to Sibelius* (London, 1987), pp. 121–2.

16　Tovey, 'Requiem', p. 202.

17　In the *Requiem* – and in general – Verdi usually uses ₵ metre as a matter of practicality, in passages moving at breakneck speed; otherwise he notates the passage in common time, even though a performance in ₵ may be called for (as in the opening of the *Dies iræ*). There is one exception to this generalization in the sacred music: the *Pater noster* of 1880 is notated in ₵ ($\quarternote$ = 60); the use of *alla breve* here is clearly an emblem of the Palestrina style. And in the operas there are a few examples where ₵ is used in a relatively slow tempo to evoke church music, if not exactly *stile antico*: for example, see the passage for 'Organo nell'interno della Chiesa' at the beginning of the final number of *Luisa Miller* and the prayer for *voci sole* in Act IV of *Aroldo*.

18　But Budden hears a 'hint at the outline' of the *Dies iræ* plainchant at the setting of the second stanza ('Solvet sæclum') of the *Dies iræ* movement (*Verdi*, p. 322). And Olin Downes perceived connections between Verdi's *Requiem* and the cues to plainchant added to his autograph manuscript for the liturgical ceremony commemorating Manzoni's death (*New York Times*, 27 May 1951). I am not convinced by either claim, but readers should judge for themselves.

19　Depictions of chant in opera are rare, but the 'Scena del giudizio' of *Aida* ('Spirto del Nume sovra noi discendi!') comes close; it is neither restricted to a single note nor 'senza misura', but is written without bar lines or clear melodic profile. In any event, it is closer to the opening of the *Te Deum* than to anything in the *Requiem*.

20　There are a few additional passages for *voci sole* which do not, however, evoke the *stile antico*: (1) 'Quid sum miser' (bb. 296–9 and 315–21), (2) 'Lacrymosa' ('Pie Jesu' section), (3) *Offertorio* (bb. 208–12), last vocal statement, (4) *Agnus Dei* (bb. 1–13), (5) *Lux æterna* (bb. 27–42):

'et lux perpetua', (6) *Libera me*: the short *falsobordone* passage in the opening section and the 'Requiem æternam' section.

21 Verdi had written a chorus in the Palestrina style for the opening of Act III, but later discarded it. Its replacement is 'O tu che sei d'Osiride', an example of his own religious topos.

Select bibliography

Abbiati, Franco. *Giuseppe Verdi.* 4 vols. (Milan 1959).

Beghelli, Marco. 'Per un nuovo approccio al teatro musicale: l'atto performativo come luogo dell'imitazione gestuale nella drammaturgia verdiana', *Italica* 64 (1987), pp. 632–53.

Budden, Julian. *Verdi,* Master Musicians (London 1985).

Bülow, Hans von. 'Musikalisches aus Italien', in Hans von Bülow, *Briefe und Schriften,* ed. Marie von Bülow. 8 vols. (Leipzig 1896–1908), vol. 3 (*Ausgewählte Schriften, 1850–1892*), pp. 340–52.

Filippi, Filippo. Review of the premiere of Verdi's *Requiem. La perseveranza,* 23 May 1874, reprinted in *La gazzetta musicale di Milano,* 24 May 1874.

Review of the first performance of Verdi's *Requiem* at La Scala. *La perseveranza,* 28 May 1874.

Gatti, Carlo. *Verdi.* 2 vols. (Milan 1931). 3rd rev. edn. in one vol. (Verona 1953). *Verdi: The Man and his Music* [English translation of the 1953 version], trans. Elisabeth Abbott (New York 1955).

Girardi, Michele, and Pierluigi Petrobelli, eds. *Messa per Rossini: La storia, il testo, la musica,* Quaderni dell'Istituto di studi verdiani, vol. V (Parma and Milan 1988).

Greene, David B. 'Giuseppe Verdi's *Dies irae*', *Response in Worship, Music, the Arts* 11 (1971), pp. 77–88.

Hanslick, Eduard. 'Verdi's Requiem', in *Musikalische Stationen* (*Die 'moderne Oper'*, Part 2) (Berlin 1880), pp. 3–12; translation in Eduard Hanslick, *Music Criticisms 1846–99,* trans. and ed. Henry Pleasants, rev. edn. (Baltimore, Maryland 1963), pp. 160–6.

Herrmann, William Albert Jr. 'Religion in the Operas of Giuseppe Verdi' (Dissertation, Columbia University 1963).

Hussey, Dyneley. *Verdi,* Master Musicians, 5th rev. edn. (London 1973).

Luzio, Alessandro, ed. *Carteggi verdiani.* 4 vols. (Rome 1935 [vols. I–II] and 1947 [vols. III–IV]).

Martin, George. 'Verdi, Manzoni, and the *Requiem*' and 'Franz Werfel and the "Verdi Renaissance"', in *Aspects of Verdi* (New York 1988), pp. 31–58 and pp. 61–77, respectively.

Monaldi, Gino. *Verdi: 1839–1898* (Turin 1899), 3rd edn. (Milan 1946).

Phillips-Matz, Mary Jane. *Verdi: A Biography* (Oxford 1993).

Pizzetti, Ildebrando. 'La religiosità di Verdi: Introduzione alla *Messa da Requiem*', *Nuova antologia* 76 (1941), pp. 209–13.

Reyer, Ernest. 'Requiem de Verdi', in *Notes de musique*, 2nd edn. (Paris 1875), pp. 358–70.

Robertson, Alec. *Requiem: Music of Mourning and Consolation* (London 1967).

Roeder, John. 'Pitch and Rhythmic Dramaturgy in Verdi's Lux æterna', *19th Century Music* 14/2 (1990), pp. 169–85.

'Formal Functions of Hypermeter in the "Dies irae" of Verdi's *Requiem*', *Theory and Practice* (forthcoming).

Roncaglia, Gino. 'Il "Requiem" di Verdi', in *Le celebrazioni del 1963 e alcune nuove indagini sulla musica italiana del XVIII e XIX secolo: Numero unico per la XX 'Settimana Musicale Senese'*, ed. Mario Fabbri et al. (Florence 1963), pp. 99–115.

Rosen, David. 'Verdi's "Liber scriptus" Rewritten', *Musical Quarterly* 55 (1969), pp. 151–69.

'The Genesis of Verdi's *Requiem*' (Dissertation, University of California at Berkeley 1976).

'La *Messa* a Rossini e il *Requiem* per Manzoni', *Rivista italiana di musicologia* 4 (1969), pp. 127–37 and 5 (1970), pp. 216–33, reprinted in *Messa per Rossini: La storia, il testo, la musica*, Quaderni dell'Istituto di studi verdiani (Parma and Milan 1988), vol. V, pp. 119–49.

'The Operatic Origins of Verdi's "Lacrymosa"', *Studi verdiani* 5 (1988–9), pp. 65–84.

'Reprise as Resolution in Verdi's *Messa da Requiem*', *Theory and Practice* (forthcoming).

Tovey, Donald Francis. 'Requiem in Memory of Manzoni', *Essays in Musical Analysis*. 6 vols. (London 1937), vol. V (*Vocal Music*), pp. 195–209.

Toye, Francis. *Giuseppe Verdi: His Life and Works* (London 1931), rev. edn. (New York 1946).

Walker, Frank. *The Man Verdi* (London 1962), repr. edn. (Chicago 1982).

Weaver, William. *Verdi: A Documentary Study* (London [1977]).

Index

Index